HUMANS OF THE WORLD MEETING OF FAMILIES

HUMANS OF THE WORLD MEETING OF FAMILIES

EDITED BY BRENDA DRUMM

Published 2020 by
Veritas Publications
7–8 Lower Abbey Street
Dublin 1, Ireland
publications@veritas.ie
www.veritas.ie

978 1 84730 889 4

10 9 8 7 6 5 4 3 2 1

A catalogue record for this book is available from the British Library.

Designed by Jeannie Swan, Veritas Publications
Printed by W&G Baird, Antrim

Veritas books are printed on paper made from the wood pulp of managed forests.
For every tree felled, at least one tree is planted, thereby renewing natural resources.

CONTENTS

HUMANS OF THE WORLD MEETING OF FAMILIES

ACKNOWLEDGEMENTS

When you come to write down the 'thank you' section there is always a danger that you will forget someone. I apologise in advance for leaving anyone out.

I want to acknowledge the following and say thank you to:

• All of the team in the World Meeting of Families 2018 Media and Communications Office: Sinéad Brennan, Pamela McLoughlin, Dearbhla Geraghty, David Macken, Katie Crosby, Robert McGivney and Tara McGahan. The Humans of the World Meeting of Families 2018 project would not have been possible without their enthusiasm and their commitment to the overall day-to-day running of what was a really busy office;

• My fellow managers in the WMOF2018 offices and to the diocesan delegates for their wonderful work and dedication to bringing this once in a lifetime event to life;

• To Fr Tim Bartlett, Secretary General of WMOF2018, and Anne Griffin, General Manager of WMOF2018;

• To colleagues in the Catholic Communications Office, Maynooth.

Dublin Diocesan Communications Office and to diocesan communications officers across the country;

• To colleagues in the Vatican press and media offices especially Matteo and Alessandro, and to colleagues in the Dicastery for Laity, Family and Life;

• To all the team at Veritas for their work on this publication;

• To Archbishop Diarmuid Martin, President and Host of WMOF2018;

• To all those who offered up their stories and opened up their lives to us and the readers of the Humans of World Meeting of Families 2018 Facebook page.

And, finally, a huge thank you to all the families who generously lent their mothers, fathers, brothers, sisters, sons and daughters to the WMOF2018 family. There were long days of work and lengthy absences from home. I thank especially my own family: my husband Bryan and our children, Emma and Cathal, for their patience throughout 2018 and for their ever-present love and support.

You might be familiar with the phenomenon that is 'Humans of New York' which began as a photography project in 2010. The initial goal was to photograph ten thousand New Yorkers on the street and to create a catalogue of the city's inhabitants. Somewhere along the way the man behind the idea, Brandon Stanton, began to interview his subjects in addition to photographing them. These portraits and the captions/ stories that accompany them became the subject of a vibrant blog and Facebook page, which now has over twenty million followers and provides a worldwide audience with daily glimpses into the lives of strangers on the streets of New York City.

The 'Humans of ...' phenomenon began to spread and here in Ireland we now have 'Humans of Dublin' and 'Humans of Longford' to name just two.

In more recent months we have seen 'Humans of New York: Refugee Stories'. This involved Brandon Stanton travelling to Jordan and Turkey to talk to twelve different Syrian refugee families from which he shared some harrowing stories.

With Ireland's hosting of the World Meeting of Families in August 2018, I thought it would be a nice idea to highlight some of the people behind the preparations for this event and so we brought 'Humans of World Meeting of Families 2018' to life on Facebook.

The plan was to put together some of the stories of the people behind the event and also try to capture the stories of some of the families, at home here in Ireland and from overseas, who would be part of the events we were putting together in August 2018.

For almost a year leading up to the World Meeting of Families, the stories of those involved were captured and catalogued.

The Facebook page has featured stories and anecdotes about family life, past and present, from staff, volunteers, diocesan and parish participants, as well as families who travelled to the events in Dublin and Knock.

All the stories we shared on the Humans of World Meeting of Families 2018 Facebook page were linked by the themes of family and faith.

These stories offered an insight into the joys and challenges; the hopes and heartaches; the love and loss; the ordinary and extraordinary people and histories that make up our families.

We are delighted to offer them to you now in book format. There are a few new stories here from individuals and families who wanted to share their post-event stories with us and these capture the size and scale of the event for those in the middle of organising it, as well as the joyful experiences that so many families had at the various events.

We hope that you enjoy our snapshot of just some of the wonderful humans who were involved in the World Meeting of Families in Dublin.

Brenda Drumm
EDITOR

MAIRE PRINTER

I am a mother and a grandmother. I have been a widow for the past thirty years. I live in Westport, which is a beautiful town in Co. Mayo in the west of Ireland.

I grew up in a very strict but loving home in Scotland. Education and faith were very important.

My father always swore there were no Irish connections in the family. After my husband, children and I came to live in Ireland thirty-three years ago, my brother decided to do a family tree history. On my father's side he discovered his people had left Belmullet in Co. Mayo in the 1800s. It's no wonder I have always felt at home in the west of Ireland.

My parents were people of deep faith and we were brought up in a Catholic home believing in a loving and merciful God. Faith and family are very important to me and prayer is really important too.

But nowadays much of the world around me is so different to what I knew growing up. My family doesn't get to meet up as often as I would like because everyone is so busy and some of my family live overseas. But I invite all the members of my family who live near me to lunch every Sunday.

I have fond memories of my husband. I always recall a story from our honeymoon. We had no money and could not afford to go away so we borrowed a house from our relatives in England to stay in for a few days. My husband discovered that a horse called Printer was running in a race and he backed it. We knew it was risky but luck was on our side and the horse won so we finished our honeymoon in Paris!

I am retired and I have plenty of time on my hands. I was looking for something to do to serve the Church because I love meeting people and I love sharing experiences with people of faith. I think I have been very blessed in my life.

My name is Maire Printer, and I volunteered for the World Meeting of Families 2018!

JINNY MALAZARTE

My name is Jinny Malazarte. I am originally from the Philippines, but now living in Drimnagh, Dublin.

I was the 2,500th person to sign up as a volunteer for the World Meeting of Families 2018. My wife, Resurreccion, and I lived in a little village in the centre of Manilla before moving to Ireland with our two children seventeen years ago. They are grown up now and have graduated.

Our daughter works as an ICU nurse in Our Lady's Children's Hospital, Crumlin, and our son is a software engineer in SAP, Citywest.

I worked as a mechanical engineer for a hydraulics company but lost my job during the recession. I went back to education though, and finished a post-graduate diploma in Science Management at the National College of Ireland.

I've just had an interview and am hoping to be called for a job. My wife, who also volunteered for the World Meeting of Families 2018, is a TCU (Transition Care Unit) nurse. Every year she goes on the Dublin Archdiocese pilgrimage to Lourdes to volunteer in the hospital.

There are lots of religions in the Philippines but we were born Catholic. The only difference I've noticed between the Church in Ireland and in the Philippines is that more families go to Mass together at home.

Over twenty years ago, I saw Pope John Paul II when he came to the Philippines. The World Meeting of Families 2018 was an amazing event for all those who attended. While I was really busy as part of the volunteer team, I also gained a once in-a-lifetime experience from it.

MICHAEL GANNON

My name is Michael Gannon. I live in Newbridge, Co. Kildare, with my parents. My brother, Eoin, and sister, Jenny, live close by. My brother is married and he has a son, aged two. He's my godson – we are very close.

I'm doing a play at the moment with Eoin. It's about a ballet dancer. There are different characters, so it will be an interesting one to do. I play many characters, including the narrator, and I'm one of the boys as well.

I also do a bit of dancing at the weekends with a friend of mine back home. I used to be involved with Counter Balance, a professional dance company in Dublin.

Religion is a big part of our family's life. When I was growing up, we would always go to Mass on a Sunday morning or a Saturday night. It was important to go. When I was growing up I had faith and I still have faith.

My sister is part of a new Gospel choir and sometimes I go to the Mass when they sing to listen to her.

I've actually met Pope Francis before in Rome in 2014. My parents came with me to the audience. It was in St Peter's Square. He came to my mam, shook her hand; then came to me, shook my hand and gave me a blessing; and came to my dad and they had a conversation.

I told him that I used to work in Vatican Radio in Rome; they made me feel very welcome there, and I got to know Rome very well.

Through my friend, and through my mam, I did an interview with the World Meeting of Families 2018 and got a six-week internship. After that, Anne Griffin (the general manager) invited me into the office and told me about a new job as an inside reporter to write stuff on my computer, put stuff up on Facebook and support the marketing team. That's my official job at the moment. I'm here two days per week.

Before this, I was at home. I was so bored. I wanted to put my name out there. I wanted to do something different for myself. I'm very pleased with my work here.

When the Pope comes, I'd like to do some ushering because I have experience of that at home. I want to

Religion is a big part of our family's life. When I was growing up, we would always go to Mass on a Sunday morning or a Saturday night. It was important to go.

meet people, to make sure everything is going okay, like a supervisor, helping people. That's what I'd like to do. After this, I'm going to Spain for two weeks on my holidays and after that I'm writing books and looking forward to the pantomime in Newbridge.

Michael not only met Pope Francis when he came to Ireland but he also participated in the closing Mass in the Phoenix Park by carrying the processional cross to and from the altar!

DAVID BRENNAN

I got married very young in my opinion. I came home to Dublin six days after I turned twenty-one and I met a wonderful woman who is now my wife. We are together forty-five years and married forty-three years.

When I got home, an old school friend of my mother's was taking her out to watch her daughter play table tennis in a big club in Dalkey – I had played table tennis in school and played it abroad for a number of years, and am a league tennis player even now – and that's where I met my wife, Geraldine, and we got married two years later.

She came from a mixed-religion family, so religion wasn't an enormous part of her family life, but she was happy to go along with me and we reared our three children as Catholic.

My mother had enormous faith. She wasn't a private prayer-mat person; she had a very, very deep faith and was an incredibly good woman. I am a Catholic; I believe in God. I wear a Miraculous Medal, which means an awful lot to me.

I lost most of my family when I was young, and so I was reared by the Vincentians. I am still in contact with the school. I feel that I owe them something, because they certainly looked after me at a time when I needed it.

My name is David Brennan, and I volunteered for the World Meeting of Families 2018 to assist in something that I regard as very necessary for the Catholic Church. It is also very good for my city, Dublin, which I love. I believe that this is something that is really important for the Church. I personally believe srongly in family; that's one of the reasons why I chose to be involved.

> My mother had enormous faith. She wasn't a private prayer-mat person; she had a very, very deep faith and was an incredibly good woman.

**RICHARD
BRENNAN**

Our family is small, but close-knit. We are very community orientated. It's about having a place to belong. I live in Ashbourne, Co. Meath, but I'm originally from Greystones, Co. Wicklow.

Everybody wants to be a part of something bigger. There's an element of that both in faith and in volunteering, so community is the tie there. There's camaraderie, there's friendship and there are bonds and relationships that are built and, in some cases, maintained for years.

There are opportunities to serve, to give back and to help others. That's really important. By the very nature of meeting people, you interact with or you come across situations or circumstances that you may not come across in your daily routine.

While education is really important – what you learn in school and textbooks – there's also the education you get from life in general. And that's part of being in a community – learning about other people and learning how to be and how to act, and looking after each other and being one big family.

I worked for an overseas development agency for six years and travelled to Ethiopia and Kenya meeting people, seeing their situations, seeing what I could do to help and how I could be a part of it.

It all ties in with how I am now as a person, how I see things and how I would like to interact with others, and the impact I'd like to have with my sphere of influence, whatever that may be, in any small way.

Very happily and luckily for me, I saw an opportunity for this once-in-a-lifetime event that could do a lot for me personally and professionally. The World Meeting of Families 2018 gave me an opportunity to work on what I think are core values: people skills, giving back and community.

My name is Richard Brennan, and I was the Volunteer Project Manager for the World Meeting of Families 2018.

People used to come to me and say: 'I don't know if I would be of any help.' But we were delighted to work with all of those who offered their time and talents to us for the various events that made up the World Meeting of Families 2018. At the centre of all we did as volunteers was offering the famous Irish welcome, the 'Céad Míle Fáilte', at all the venues, all events, including at the airport to welcome people into the country.

There are opportunities to serve, to give back and to help others. That's really important.

BRIAN FARRELL

My claim to fame is being in the same school year as former Irish international soccer player, Damien Duff. Even then, he was a gifted footballer and could breeze through eleven players on a mazy run. He soon swapped De La Salle College, Churchtown, for Blackburn Rovers – and the rest, as they say, is history.

In the 1980s, the Dublin suburb I grew up in was known as an unholy place but, to me, it was home. Perhaps the most famous icon near my housing estate was the HB Ice Cream factory and later Premier Dairies, when it took over the Hughes Brothers' milk business. It was a big local employer and every time I see a Brunch ice cream, with its biscuity crumb coating, it takes me right back!

For many years, I worked locally in the old Braemor Rooms and later Ballinteer. Then, like a lot of the so-called 'Generation X', I packed my bags and headed to Australasia. First spending four years in New Zealand then another four in Australia.

While in Australia, I met my Malaysian wife, Chilie, while fruit picking! When you find a person that loves you for who you are, it's amazing.

The theme for the ninth World Meeting of Families was 'Joy for the World'. To me, the meaning of the word 'joy' is the emotion of great delight or happiness caused by something exceptionally good or satisfying. This event will, undoubtedly, leave a legacy of joy behind. We cannot change the past but what we can do is live in the present and bring happiness and joy to ourselves and others around us in the future.

I am Brian Farrell, a presenter on Spirit Radio, and I volunteered with the meet and greet team for the World Meeting of Families 2018. I've never volunteered for anything before, but to be involved with such an historic and feel-good event in my own country was not something to be missed.

MONICA HEMPENSTALL

My mum died when I was young, but she instilled faith in us. We grew up with the Rosary in the house and going to Mass. And, because of my loss when I was so young, my faith grew with me and I am still a practising Catholic.

I do have high moral standards, but I feel that, in today's world, you need that. Faith comes from the home and it's also taught in schools, but grandparents or aunts and uncles can influence a child's life too.

I don't think I could have gotten through my life without my faith. It's part of my life; I couldn't live without it. It gives me my purpose for my life and being involved in the World Meeting of Families 2018 felt all the more powerful because I was actually doing something and it was for my faith as well.

I worked for forty-one years in finance, but my work with the World Meeting of Families 2018 was completely different. It was a learning curve for me. It's very important to know that participation, no matter how small, is worthwhile.

All age groups, from young to old and people from abroad who are living in Ireland, wanted to be volunteers. I think it increased the community spirit and that's what we want – that's what we need. We got a group of volunteers together from my own parish – there was such excitement and a sense of community.

The volunteers were fantastic. They were from all walks of life and the camaraderie was great. At the end of the day there's a satisfaction in what we achieved.

My name is Monica Hempenstall, and I was a liaison officer processing volunteer applications for the World Meeting of Families 2018.

The volunteers were fantastic. They were from all walks of life and the camaraderie was great.

CLAIRE RUDD

I grew up in a small village in Kerry and in the early 1900s there was a telecommunications hub there linking Europe to the USA by cable. My grandfather was the first station master and my uncle was the last, as the advent of telephony meant the end of the cable era. Many of the houses are still inhabited and the area is steeped in history.

Life is very different now for me, living in a town with all of the facilities and activities on our doorstep. Our lives seem much busier now. Back then, growing up in Kerry, we only had one TV channel so we spent more time together as a family.

Liam and I are married twenty-five years this year and we have three children, Ciaran (17), Grainne (15) and Doireann (almost 12).

We've always gone to Mass and brought the children too – which can be challenging at times! I suppose the importance of faith arose when our eldest was starting school.

I love Taizé music and find myself singing (badly) as a form of prayer. We tend to be more individual, rather than pray as a family, and this is something I've become more aware of while facilitating parish conversations around family. I often pop into the church and light candles for special intentions with our children – their grandmother was a big believer in the lighting of candles and one is always lit for her.

When I met my husband's family for the first time, his mum told me about how they had travelled to Galway to see Pope John Paul II in 1979. After telling me all about the Mass and the trip and how special it was, she asked if I'd like to see their photograph of the day. Of course I said yes, expecting to see a picture of the Pope. Instead it was the family sat by the car having a picnic!

My name is Claire Rudd, and I volunteered for the World Meeting of Families 2018 because it was a once-in-a-lifetime opportunity. I had never heard of World Meeting of Families 2018 before I was asked to be on my parish committee, so it offered a great chance to a part of it. I also prefer to be active in the community and I believe in helping out where I can.

I've met so many great people since getting involved in the parish committee. Back in 1979, I had to stay at home and I watched Pope John Paul II on the telly, so I really wanted to be actively involved and present this time.

I often pop into the church and light candles for special intentions with our children – their grandmother was a big believer in the lighting of candles and one is always lit for her.

MARTIN LYNCH

I met my wife, Paula, at an international scout jamboree in Kilkenny. She was running the Red Cross centre at the camp, spotted me and said, 'That's the fella I'm going to marry' ... and she did. That was four children ago!

We are forty years married now. We were married a fortnight after the Pope was here in 1979 and we have great memories of that visit. She was the third in command of the Red Cross centre in the Phoenix Park. She was down at the hospital, the opposite end of the field to the Pope. I kind of cheated, because I hadn't volunteered as such, but I had a very good friend who was involved and he knew of a last-minute opportunity. He said, 'Martin, come over here and I'll fix you up.'

We ended up being very close to where the helicopter landed in the Phoenix Park. We got to see Pope John Paul II getting off the helicopter. In those days, people tended to behave themselves at large events and so there was a relaxed approach to the various cordons that were in place.

This was two years before Pope John Paul II was shot – in 1979 he was very vigorous; he was a real young man, an ex-soccer player and an ex-skier.

My wife had the only major casualty of the day in the Phoenix Park. The poor, unfortunate man died at about 3 a.m. as the crowds were starting to gather in the Park. Based on statistics, they were expecting about fifteen people to die, because there was a million people in the Park that day.

The organisers had opened up the hospitals to have beds available for any casualty from the Park. My wife's father had seriously injured himself and was recovering in hospital in the days leading up to the papal visit. He was discharged from hospital before the Pope arrived in Ireland. We were grateful for his discharge from hospital, in part because it meant that he could walk his daughter down the aisle – otherwise he'd still have been in hospital two weeks later during our wedding.

My dad was very strong on faith. He attributed his survival during the Second

World War to the Rosary. He had a pub in central London and stayed for the Blitz and the flying bombs. One bomb got him, and one rocket got him, but, on both occasions, he more than survived.

He was to be inducted into the Tank Corps but had an accident, which cracked up his leg extremely badly, so he didn't end up in Normandy, where the Tank Corps were cut to pieces.

He attributed his fate to the influence of the Rosary so we'd say the Rosary every night. Faith was very strong in me from an early age. I did my best with my own children, but I wasn't anywhere as successful as him! But religion does seem to inform their behaviour.

One particular son is like a Capuchin Friar: he's actually very poor himself, but seems to attract every poor and unfortunate soul. He has a soft and docile attitude to looking after them and seems to have that magnetic appeal. That makes me proud.

My name is Martin Lynch, and I volunteered for the World Meeting of Families 2018!

My dad was very strong on faith. He attributed his survival during the Second World War to the Rosary.

MICHAEL FLEMING

I remember, as a child, the many times that my viewing of the programme *Robin Hood* got delayed while we finished off a decade of the Rosary!

We said it pretty much every day – maybe not at the weekends, strangely enough, when I think about it now. We were down on our knees, trying to lean on a sofa, and I had to have my back turned to the television, even though it was turned off.

There was no recording or pausing TV shows then, so if the Rosary over-ran you missed it, and that was that.

I grew up in Coleraine, which was on a diocesan boundary. I spent my first few years on the Derry side and then moved to the other side of the river.

In those days, diocesan boundaries were important. I remember the parish priest encouraging my sisters to go to a different convent, because they were going to one on a different side of the river and in a different parish.

I met my wife, Eithne, through a mutual friend who was a work colleague of hers in the Royal Victoria

Hospital in Belfast. Our first date was to a rotary ball and she had thought rotary was something to do with watches!

She was a midwife many years ago, but her phrase is that she went to the other side of the bed when we had our three children.

Without thinking, we automatically carried on what our parents, and their parents before them, would have done, without any great debate about it. From an early age, our children would have been taught their prayers, most definitely by their mother, and they went to a Catholic primary school.

The secondary school they went to, while technically a Catholic grammar school, is actually quite mixed. It attracts people from, as the principal would say, 'all religions and none'. He's very proud of that. It's the only Dominican College in the North that has boys and girls, and that was done thirty years ago, mainly to try and establish enough numbers.

There are two or three all-girls schools still in Belfast but in our part of the world there wouldn't have been enough people to justify an all-girls school.

My name is Michael Fleming, and I volunteered for the World Meeting of Families 2018 for over a year. I travelled down once a week from Ballymoney, which is eight miles from the coast in the North of Ireland. I used to leave home at 6.15 a.m., get a train at 6.30 a.m. to Belfast, transfer across the platform to the Enterprise, get into Dublin at 10.05 a.m., and then walk around to Gardiner Street and get a bus to Drumcondra.

I enjoyed it; it was very different. They had me doing a lot of data entry and follow-ups, and it was nice to see the applicants processed and accepted. Obviously, the work load increased as we moved closer to the events. I initially planned to volunteer until the end of the events in August, but my wife thought I'd be there for the whole month of August, never mind just the week itself. (She was right!)

Without thinking, we automatically carried on what our parents, and their parents before them, would have done, without any great debate about it.

CONN McNALLY

We are very committed to eating together as a family – that would be the primary way that we stay up-to-date with each other. We have a dog, so we bring the dog out places, such as beaches and parks. Unfortunately, it can be difficult for us all to go together as both my dad and I work full time.

Probably the biggest change in family life was when my older brother moved abroad. He is currently living in Edinburgh, where he works. Another upcoming change will be his marriage at the end of May. This will obviously change the dynamic in our family as it expands to include another person.

Faith plays a very important role in my life. Being connected to an eternal truth that transcends whatever happens to be in vogue at the moment gives a great deal of meaning and joy in life.

The importance of faith for members of my family varies significantly. At one end, there are those for whom their faith is the most important thing in their life. On the other end, there are those who never think about religion.

There would also be family members somewhere in-between.

Prayer is something that I do regard as being of importance. It is something that I certainly must work on a bit more. Specifically, I think I'm the opposite to a lot of people who may only pray in times of need. If I am going through something difficult, I lose the inclination to pray – it is something I'm trying to work on.

I hold a Master of Philosophy in Classics degree from Trinity College Dublin. I had previously completed my BA in Ancient and Medieval History and Culture in Trinity as well. I am particularly interested in Late Roman Archaeology.

My Master's thesis was on Late Western Roman Consular Diptychs – it is such an obscure topic that people either ask a million questions or ask nothing! My undergraduate dissertation was on the effectiveness of current methodologies in calculating population sizes in the Roman world.

I am currently trying to decide whether or not to do a PhD. I am not certain what I would do specifically, but I am certain if I were to do it my thesis would be on something in Late Roman Archaeology.

My name is Conn McNally, and I worked in office support for the World Meeting of Families 2018.

I was born in Co. Monaghan, but we moved to Dublin in 1944 when I was two. My mother wasn't well. She got pleurisy, and the family farm was going downhill, so my family decided to leave. But my father regretted it as long as he lived. He didn't like city life. It wasn't his style at all. I think it was a bad move from Daddy and Mammy's point of view.

He worked in CIE when he moved to Dublin and it was very difficult for a man who was used to the country way of life to settle in here.

I got a job in the Bon Secours Hospital in Glasnevin as a laboratory technician, as the hospital had a connection to my school. There was a nun there, Sr Bernadette, and she had a huge influence on my life.

I loved it in the lab. Sr Bernadette mostly took the bloods, but we all did at times – we received marvellous training. We did blood counts and were literally counting the cells under the microscope. Everything now is 'press a button'.

The nuns were very frugal; very little was disposable and that probably influenced my life. I must be the only person that recycles every scrap of paper and plastic that comes into the house.

I met my husband, Tom, in the Legion of Mary. I had my eye on him, but I didn't know if he was single or not, as he was a bit older than I was. I fancied him though, and we were always chatting. He drove me home one night and we started dating from there. We were fifty years married in September.

He's sixteen years older than me, but it has never made any difference. He's fitter than I am! There were nine children in his family. He was the eldest boy and left school when he was fourteen. If you think back eighty years ago, the country was in an awful state with very little money and high unemployment. But he educated himself and worked hard to make it to all the way up in the civil service.

He took early retirement in 1991 but has kept himself fully occupied and the day isn't long enough for him. We usually go to ten o'clock morning Mass

together, and then we come home, have a cup of tea, he might read the paper and I might go off. We have a camper van and we spend a lot of time on trips in that.

We have five children. One daughter is halfway through her first pregnancy. She was asking me for advice at the weekend. I said: 'You'll be fine. We'll all help you. Once you keep the baby clean and dried and fed, they rear themselves – and loads of love; you can't love them enough.'

I was in the Phoenix Park when Pope John Paul II visited in 1979. I'll never forget it. Tom was at home with our three girls and I took the boys. My sister lived beside the Phoenix Park so we stayed there the night before.

When his helicopter went over the crowd, a nun beside me fell on her knees with joy. I'll never forget it. That was the highlight of the day, seeing him arrive in the helicopter right overhead.

When I came home, Tom went off to see the Pope in Knock with the Knock Shrine Bureau and he didn't come back until about 4 a.m. They went in coaches, but they couldn't turn them around on the narrow streets, so they were all stuck, but it didn't matter as everyone was so happy. There was a joke for weeks afterwards that people were still trying to get back from Knock!

My name is Sarah Gurrie, and I was a volunteer for the World Meeting of Families. I used to go into the office every Tuesday and I helped look after the volunteers and staff. I was available anywhere I was needed. If anything had to be done, I did it, and that's what I like to do.

FATHER EAMONN MCCARTHY

I am one of six siblings, three girls and three boys, and grew up in Cork City. One of the novelties was the key left in everyone's front door. In our little cul-de-sac of sixteen homes, there were about sixty children, from teenagers to toddlers, and we had no end of on-street fun and, of course, mischief!

Having graduated as a civil engineer from UCC in the 1980s, when work was scarce, I spent seven years working on building sites in London, and came home as a chartered quantity surveyor, only to pack it all in and head for the seminary in Maynooth.

The fact that my brother and I are both diocesan priests speaks to the importance of our faith growing up. Sunday Mass and the family Rosary were encouraged strongly, but I never remember undue pressure being applied. It was considered a normal part of family activity.

Looking back, it has certainly sustained us through many a rough patch and it most certainly has kept us a well-united family too, even though we are now geographically scattered.

Statues and holy images were always the norm at home. The holy water font is still never allowed to run dry and it is now hung a little lower down the wall for the younger children to reach. These days, gathering as a family for Sunday dinner at one of my sister's homes is always a good way to keep in touch.

One of my nephews has been accepted for training for the priesthood for the Diocese of Arlington in Virginia, USA. He has a third uncle a diocesan priest on his father's side, so he had no chance!

Just recently, I popped into my home parish church in Ballinlough, Cork City – where I was baptised, made my First Holy Communion and received Confirmation – to say a prayer. There was a lovely prayerful ambiance there, the smell of home and a strong sense of the 'real presence' always.

I bumped into a local couple and I took the opportunity to thank an old friend of mine, Mairín, for a seed she had sown twenty years previously. She was taken aback to learn that

Statues and holy images were always the norm at home. The holy water font is still never allowed to run dry and it is now hung a little lower down the wall for the younger children to reach.

her compliment about the quality of my speaking voice, following the celebration of my first Mass after ordination, would bear fruit. It led me to an interest in radio broadcasting and eventually to a full-time involvement in the world family of Radio Maria and its ministry – the power of a kindly spoken word from my parish family to a global family of seventy-seven radio stations in seventy different countries!

A recent visit to Germany as part of my work allowed me to see the incredible generosity of so many wonderful Catholics there in support of Radio Maria Ireland – each radio station hosts an annual 'Mariathon', or fundraiser, to assist a new or growing sister station.

The faith and kindness I witnessed was made all the more poignant by the fact that an uncle of mine was killed by a German landmine in North Africa in 1943, leaving behind a young widow and two children. It brought much pain and suffering upon my extended family, not least through my father who lamented always such a tremendous 'waste' of human life.

How sad that the influence of this one loss visited upon my own family can be multiplied so many times over. How precious is life; how sacred is the family!

I currently reside with the Spiritan Fathers in Kimmage Manor, Dublin, although I am a diocesan priest from the Diocese of Cloyne, Co. Cork.

Kimmage Manor serves what were formerly known as the Holy Ghost Fathers. I am a guest of this once-flourishing religious order among a group of around eighty men who have served in Africa and Latin America, and from Alaska to Australia. Breakfast table conversations can be very intriguing!

My name is Fr Eamonn McCarthy, Priest Director of Radio Maria Ireland, and we were delighted to share the good news about the World Meeting of Families 2018 through our broadcast networks.

When I was growing up in Dublin, the family unit was very united, but I prefer the family of today. Simply because, when people emigrated in the 1980s, it was a dreadful wrench on the family unit. Families were connected in different ways back then but now, thankfully, they are united despite any distance. Thanks to Skype and social media, the world is much smaller.

I'm not saying it's not still hard to leave home, but there are more and more ways for families to be united, from a technological point of view. We have several families in St Michan's Parish who are separated by distance but, whether they live in Australia, the US, or the UK, they are connecting much easier now.

I grew up in Rialto, Kimmage, and Kilnamanagh, as the eldest of seven children. We were Sunday Mass-goers, and we tried the family Rosary to some modest success growing up. We were an ordinary suburban Dublin family at a time when people hadn't an awful lot. It might be a cliché to say it, but we were happy. There were a lot of challenges in the Ireland of the 1970s and 1980s, though, with recession, lots of unemployment, and a lot of lads I grew up with decided to go to the UK and US.

My dad was laid off in the 1980s, and it was difficult for him to get another job as employers wanted to take on younger lads. For a while, he got some work with a company in Wales, so he travelled over and back. I remember he'd send a few bob home. Even though we were all aware of it, it affected my mam most. I do remember some of the challenges, such as borrowing cigarettes or sugar from the neighbour next door 'until Friday'.

Margaret, the lady next door, also collected money for what we called 'The Frawley's Club'. Frawley's was a big department store on Thomas Street and it dressed us all every Christmas through the money my mother had set aside during the year.

I went to school in Synge Street CBS and did my Leaving Cert in 1987. I joined the Capuchin Order straight after it. I studied theology and philosophy, then

**FATHER
BRYAN
SHORTALL
OFM CAP**

I did an MA in School Chaplaincy and spent ten years working in schools, three years as a chaplain to Beaumont Hospital, and then the last eight years as parish priest in St Michan's, in Dublin's 'Law Quarter'.

We have a fantastic community of all ages and stories. There are a lot of difficulties but, despite these, people are not giving in to negativity. Many have huge cause to be sad about the difficulties they face, but they don't cave in because of the great spirit of family they have. They are a wonderful group.

The families in the parish are the kind we talk about and reminisce about when we were small: kids being able to go into each other's houses, the kettle always on, the fire lit. I often call the members of the local community 'the extended family' because they literally live next door to each other.

The parish celebrated its bicentenary last year, and we had some wonderful experiences of family and of community. We had a parish visitation, where we went around to the different parts of the parish, and many came out to meet us. There was bunting, tea and coffee, cakes, and little altars. People were really welcoming and we got to meet some parishioners who aren't able to get out and about as much as they used to, and we were able to celebrate the Sacrament of the Sick with them.

My name is Bryan Shortall, and I am a Capuchin Franciscan. I was parish priest of St Michan's during the World Meeting of Families, which was one of the churches that was featured in the Dublin Diocesan World Meeting of Families pilgrim walk.

Richard: I had a stroke three years ago, totally out of the blue. I was healthy up to that point – at least I thought I was.

I wasn't in employment at the time, but I was involved in the GAA and the musical society in Trim – I was working harder than I ever did when I was being paid! Every day was a day of adventure.

One morning, I didn't feel great so I stayed in bed for a while. At about 11.30 a.m., I felt funny. I tried to get up but I wasn't able. Luckily, I was in bed – I could have been out in the car or in the garden. People called to me that day and they couldn't understand why I wasn't answering the door, with the car parked outside.

Mary came home from work at 5.30 p.m. She knew something was wrong. I was brought to Navan Hospital and they did marvellous work there. The forecast at one stage was that I would die, but I made a great recovery, except for my right-hand side; but I can talk and I go swimming.

Amazingly, I can stand on my own in the water; I can move up and down from one end of the pool to the other. In the water, my right leg works, but I can't move it out of the water.

Mary: Prayer was massive in Richard's recovery. We are convinced that the power of prayer got us through this. Everybody was praying for him; the amount of Mass cards he got was amazing. People were huge-hearted. He has enough Rosary beads to start up a society.

It's sad now that some families have no religion, and you'd wonder what they turn to when they face difficulties. It's really important to have something; it certainly meant a lot to us when he got sick.

We met through Macra Na Feirme here in Dublin. We were both in the same club and were involved in Macra for about a year or more before we started going out. We got married thirty years ago this year, in 1988, four years after we first started going out together.

Richard: My sister and I set out from our home in Whitehall that morning – it was quite dark – and we walked the whole way in to the Phoenix Park. It was a great experience. The Pope went up and down in the popemobile, so we got quite near him. It was a great occasion – a million people together – it was extraordinary.

We are Richard and Mary Harrahill, and we volunteered together for the World Meeting of Families 2018.

We had very similar backgrounds, which was a great thing – rather than one being religious and one not. We go to Mass every Sunday and on feast days; we work in the parish and we try to say the Rosary every night.

We both went to see Pope John Paul II separately when he visited Ireland in 1979.

I went to Galway, because that's where the Youth Mass was being celebrated. We got the train up from Kerry and travelled overnight. We watched the helicopter coming in – it was a little dot in the sky. There was such excitement.

It's sad now that some families have no religion, and you'd wonder what they turn to when they face difficulties. It's really important to have something; it certainly meant a lot to us when he got sick.

EILISH MURPHY

I got a job in the civil service in May 1970, a month before my Leaving Cert – once you got a good pensionable job in those days, you thought you had to take it. I got time off to go home to Cavan for the exams, though.

My sister had started working in Guinness just before me, so we moved to Dublin together. We stayed in the Sisters of Charity hostel on Mountjoy Square until we got a flat together.

If you weren't in by midnight at the weekends, you were locked out of the hostel, even though the dances weren't over until 1 a.m. Occasionally we would get permission to be out until 1 a.m., but most weekends we'd actually go home to Cavan. We couldn't really afford to pay the bus fare though, so we'd hitch a lift!

When I started working, I was earning ten pounds per week, and the hostel cost about five pounds, so we had very little money.

We grew up in a very Catholic family; we had devotions every Sunday evening, Confession every month, and we wouldn't come down in the morning without having said our morning prayers.

When we were small, our grandmother was living with us, so we'd say the Rosary every evening, down on our knees on cement floors. There were no cushions allowed – you'd dirty them if you put them on the floor!

I met my husband, Robert, at a dance in the National Ballroom at the top of Parnell Square in Dublin. I was a few years in Dublin at the time. He asked me to dance. That was the way it was done then – the women would have been on one side of the hall, and the men on the other, and they crossed over and back.

When we decided that we were getting married, we bought a house in 1977. I was renting in Glasnevin at the time, and I continued living there while my husband moved out to the new house in Ashbourne on his own. He lived there on his own until we got married the following year.

Our four children cannot understand why I didn't go out and live with him, but that was the way it was done then.

My name is Eilish Murphy, and I volunteered with the World Meeting of Families from June 2017 to August 2018.

MARIANA SLOWETZKY

I met my husband, Toly, in Brazil when I was eleven. He's from my neighbourhood. We became friends, and now we've been married for five years. We have a twenty-month-old daughter, Clarissa, who was named after the St Clare of Assisi congregation. I am also a Catholic singer, with a full album recorded in Portuguese and English.

We have been in Ireland since 2012. I initially came here to learn English and was supposed to stay for just one year, but we liked the country and the people so much that we decided to stay.

You can't compare the Catholic Church in Brazil to Ireland because we have a population of 207 million people. In general, the Catholic Church in Brazil is very young, where a high percentage of the congregation consists of young people. I was there recently and it was very common to see churches full with four hundred to five hundred young people for prayer groups.

We are a very charismatic country in that sense; we try to do our best by having a 'young heart' and to attract young people, so we have lots of live music and drama and so on, and young priests as well.

In some places, the average age for a priest in parishes is twenty-five to twenty-eight years old, and that attracts young people a lot, who believe that living by example is more powerful than words. The Church in Brazil is still very traditional though.

We were delighted to see someone from South America being elected Pope. It was very uplifting, and it helps the Church a lot, not just in Argentina, but in South America as a whole. It attracts a lot of young people who look to Pope Francis as an inspiration for life and faith, so that helped a lot to increase the faith in Brazil. Lots of people also returned to the Church after World Youth Day 2013 and seeing the Pope's acts of love around the country.

My name is Mariana Slowetzky, and I worked as a volunteer co-ordinator with the volunteer team for the World Meeting of Families 2018.

MARY JACKSON

I volunteered in the offices of the World Meeting of Families 2018 for over a year. I might never have volunteered if my gran hadn't shared the story of a treasured photograph of Mam in her First Holy Communion dress, which she wore to the 1932 Eucharistic Congress.

She had made her First Holy Communion that year, and my nephew made his last week, and he was overheard saying to his little friend: 'Aren't we so lucky that the Pope is coming to Ireland the year we are making our First Holy Communion!'

His school had asked for old photos and my sister asked me to root out that one of our mother, which was then put up on display on the ambo during the ceremony.

Being a Catholic has always been important to me and some of my best memories are of Church-related events. I am very grateful to my late parents, Colm and Nancy, and maternal grandparents, Bessie and Joe, who passed on their faith to me.

People nowadays say they are very spiritual, but that's not what Catholicism

was back then – it was the public expression, going to Mass, saying the Rosary; the community element was very important.

For my mother and her family, turning out for a very large event like the Eucharistic Congress in 1932, where everybody was celebrating, gave them a lot of comfort and support.

When Pope John Paul II visited the Phoenix Park in 1979, I saw him only in the distance, but that didn't matter; what mattered was that you were a part of it.

I often say to people that I've over fifty years' experience in volunteering! My sisters and I were roped in early, aged about ten, to wash dishes at parish 'sales of work' in the national school in Monkstown. My mother and grandmother would be outside, pushing the sales, and we'd do our bit in the kitchen.

I'm very fortunate to have been influenced by some great people, including teachers at school and the parish clergy, nuns and lay people I've worked with as a volunteer over the years.

It's not just my personal faith that I'm thinking about, but about how much more meaningful it is when we come together to share, pray and work as a community.

People nowadays say they are very spiritual, but that's not what Catholicism was back then – it was the public expression, going to Mass, saying the Rosary; the community element was very important.

DAVID KENNEDY

I can count my cousins without using all of my fingers, but my fiancée Fiona's family is massive. They are more like a clan. There are so many cousins, uncles, aunties, in-laws, nieces, and nephews. All of this has greatly enriched my family life – not that it was impoverished before – it's just great to know that you have something good to ground you in life.

We met in college nearly ten years ago. She had called over with friends to my place and we got talking. As the conversation flowed, the matter of our ages came up, particularly birthdays. I told her that I was nineteen and that I was born in August, to which she replied that she too was nineteen and born in August. I asked her what date in August and she said it was the sixteenth – the same day I was born.

I thought that she was lying and that one of the lads must have been messing with me. So, in the course of this argument, she asked me to show her proof. We went to grab my driver's licence from my bag in my room. It turned out no one was messing with me; we were born on the exact same day only hours apart and the course of that conversation led to our first kiss. Nine years later, we are engaged and due to marry next year.

Life presents the reality of God in a profound way. Family, where love is at the centre, is the heart and life of society and the Church. It presents the fabric or thread from which all our other relationships are made.

I will never forget the first time my friends came to my house and encountered my uncle Tom. I will never forget the shock on their faces as they watched him herding cattle down the field by himself. Why? Well, Tom is blind!

Faith is something that has been around me my whole life, through my family – both explicitly and implicitly. I think the manner in which that faith manifests itself in my family varies but, no matter the manner of expression it takes, it's there and it is valued for being there.

In everyday life, prayer is also important. It gives me strength and it centres me in what can be – at the best of times – a chaotic world. The type of prayer varies from simple prayers in the morning, at meal time and at the end of the day, to more meditative prayer using silence dynamically or reading the Divine Office.

I was most looking forward to the international dimension of the World Meeting of Families 2018 – for the young people of Ireland to encounter other young people from around the world who aren't afraid to celebrate their faith and are joyful about it.

I am David Kennedy from Co. Kilkenny, and I was a researcher with the World Meeting of Families 2018.

PEGGY O'SULLIVAN

When I left college, I went to Africa on 'Her Majesty's Service' and I was paid a fortune. Kenya wasn't long independent, and there was a shortage of science teachers, so I went as part of British Aid.

It was awful getting paid this enormous amount of money as the African teachers in the same school were getting a low salary. After that, I went back as a volunteer and I spent five years in Kenya and six years in Sudan. You really do get more than you give; that's the Gospel truth.

I was working in Kenya as a science teacher in 1968 when the school decided that they wanted to teach A-level scripture, but they had nobody to teach it. Whether I volunteered or I was asked, I have no idea, but I started teaching scripture and it was wonderful.

I had attended a lecture given by Dr Dermot Ryan, later Archbishop of Dublin, on the prophets Amos and Hosea, and that was the sum total of my biblical knowledge when I started teaching scripture. But, I read all around it in preparation for the classes, and then I thought: this is it. I just loved it. I'm from Cork originally, but my father was in the army and was transferred to Dublin in 1960.

We were one of these families who weren't religious in the normal sense of the word. My mother would try and get us to say the Rosary and it would last for about two nights, and that was it for the next few years. We weren't conventionally religious, but there was clearly something there.

My father was always campaigning, doing things to make sure that other people got something. I remember there was something about pensions, that some people weren't applying for them, and him making sure that they did. He had a lot of community interests, and was in a lot of bodies, like the GAA, and always volunteering. I suppose that rubbed off on me.

My name is Peggy O'Sullivan, and I volunteered for the World Meeting of Families 2018. I loved the whole idea of it. I'm retired, I'm interested in the Church and I wanted to make a contribution.

My mother would try and get us to say the Rosary and it would last for about two nights, and that was it for the next few years. We weren't conventionally religious, but there was clearly something there.

CATHERINE MOLONEY

I've been a widow for the last nine years. Our youngest son was only twelve when my husband, David, died suddenly at just fifty-five. Our son had made his Confirmation four weeks beforehand, and then we were in the same church for the funeral, but I'm grateful David had been there for it. He had been a fit, healthy man; he never smoked, and played tennis and golf.

I met him when I was in fifth year in school. We broke up, and then I went on holidays to Kerry, but as I was walking

through Tralee one day I bumped into him, and that was it. We were married in July 1979 and went to the Phoenix Park to see Pope John Paul II as a young married couple. We have three children and I've just become a grandmother to Cúan – the translation from Irish is 'little wolf'!

I volunteered with the World Meeting of Families 2018 for over two years, helping find host families for people from abroad who wanted to be part of the event but couldn't do so unless there was some assistance. The requests came in from all over the world. And, looking at the hotel prices, the cost of accommodation was prohibitive for a lot of them to travel.

For that reason, we tried to open it up to as many people as we could by requesting host families who had a spare room and access to public transport into Dublin city centre to come forward. We were not looking for hotel standards, just a bed, with a breakfast to start them off for the day, between 20 and 27 August. Those in need were divided into three groups: individuals; couples; and couples with children.

We tried to house the largest groups first and work our way down from there. At one point we had one group of 268 from Toledo in Spain. We tried to host them close together in one or two parishes, rather than having them scattered all around Dublin.

Each applicant needed to get a letter from their own bishop to say that they are known and are okay to travel, so host families could be assured that all requests went through a system.

I first started getting involved with this type of work with the Special Olympics in 2003. The organisers were looking for hosts for the families of athletes in all parts of the country.

Then I put my name down for the International Eucharistic Congress in 2012, when two of us co-ordinated the hosting side. Everything went well, and it was a great experience, but that was over a three-day event – the World Meeting of Families was probably ten or fifteen times bigger than that. When I came on board, though, I was grateful for the background I had. At least I came in knowing a fair bit about what had occurred at the last two events and the possible pit falls, and was able to put a system in place so that it would go smoothly.

My name is Catherine Moloney, and I was a volunteer for the World Meeting of Families 2018.

I volunteered with the World Meeting of Families 2018 for over two years, helping find host families for people from abroad who wanted to be part of the event ...

EFREN AND MARIVEL BAGARES

We met in Iligan City, in the Philippines, when Efren was in university and was boarding in my friend's house. I was fourteen at the time and used to pass that house on my way to school every day!

I come from a broken family and I prayed that God would give us enlightenment. And that if I were to have my own family, that it would be a happy home.

We got married on 12 May 1990. We have four children, two of them were born in the Philippines, and the younger ones in Ireland. When we go home to visit family, they are eager to come back here – their life is here, so maybe we will stay!

Having the whole family in Ireland is a great challenge for us as parents due to differences in cultural, economic, social and spiritual matters. Our two grown children are no longer active in their faith and, in fact, our eldest son has started to ask questions about the reality of faith and the existence of Christ. So, it is a big challenge for us, as we are very active in the global religious movement 'Couples for Christ'. All our concerns are raised to God through our prayers and in the Holy Eucharist.

For us, prayer is very important because this is where we can express our praise, thanksgiving, send all our heavy loads and ask for strength and hope on our way forward. Every day, before going out, we start with a prayer and everything throughout the day is fine.

We believe that the family is very important as a basic unit of society, and as the heart of the Church, and it needs to be strengthened as the modern world we live in can affect our faith.

There are two hundred couples in Couples for Christ groups across the island of Ireland which meet twice monthly to pray for one another. It strengthens our faith.

We are Efren and Marivel Bagares, and we volunteered as a host family for the World Meeting of Families 2018. We have a two-bed apartment in the centre of Dublin and vacated our bedroom to host a couple. We slept in the sitting room on a blow-up mattress. That is our practice, whenever friends come to stay.

The World Meeting of Families 2018 was a global call to all of us to gather together as one big family of Christ. We look forward to the ongoing transformation of all families, moved by the Holy Spirit, that will renew the face of the earth.

FATHER PIOTR GALUS

I was a teenager when I met Pope John Paul II, when he came to say Mass as Cardinal of Krakow. I remember my father saying, 'He will be somebody important for the Polish Church, because he has a strong personality.' Two years later, he was elected Pope.

I grew up in a rural part of Poland where we had a farm, and everyone worked very hard. My family was always very religious: my mother's two sisters were nuns, and we had a cousin who was a priest. As far back as I can remember, prayers, Sunday Mass and visiting the cemeteries were always part of our life.

I have been living in Cork for the last twelve years, and am chaplain to the Polish community. I celebrate two Masses on Sundays, at 10 a.m. and 6 p.m., which are attended by about eight hundred people. I cover the whole diocese for the preparation of marriage. Most get married in Poland, but the preparation and documentation is done in Cork. Also, I cover baptisms, visits to the hospitals and house visits.

My name is Fr Piotr Galus, and I am responsible for a movement of families called the 'Domestic Church', similar to Teams of Our Lady. We started-up in Ireland five years ago, although the movement in Poland is nearly fifty years old. There are twenty-five groups of families involved in Ireland, who meet once per month for three hours.

I've been with these families for five years and I can see how they are growing spiritually and that they are people I can trust and are ready to help me. They are growing in spirit. They want to share this, to help other people, to become closer to God and closer to the Church.

In Poland, every school has two hours of religious education per week, but it is mostly taught by priests and nuns. I can say that this often does not work best for the family. Children from the families of the Domestic Church may have less knowledge of religion, but they are closer to God.

In my experience, the hours of teaching in school are hopeless, they don't help.

However, if the child sees their parents kneeling for prayer, going to Confession, going every Sunday to Church, you can see that it helps them to be nice to each other. It's the best catechism for the child.

Through the relationship between the parents, the child discovers their relationship with God, because it's almost the same – God is family. Because of that, I'm very happy to be involved with this movement. I can hear how the children, maybe just three or four years old, can make up their own prayers – not just a Hail Mary – they can ask for forgiveness from God, they pray for their father and mother's health, or other children starving in Africa.

If you help families, or a couple, you help everyone, because they are like a priest or prophet in their own homes.

SARAH AND DECLAN O'BRIEN

We were married a few years when we realised there was something missing - our lives were so busy with our young children, we'd get to Mass, but not even together, and we were constantly on the go. We were vaguely aware that the void was in the spiritual area. We had a friend, Fr Tom Norris, who was part of the Focolare Movement and he put us in touch with another couple.

We started going along to the Word of Life meetings, where we looked at a particular passage from the Gospel and learned how ordinary people like ourselves could put the teachings into practice.

At the beginning, we failed, we made mistakes and we weren't perfect parents, but we did the best for our children. After a year or two, we realised that what was missing had actually been the presence of Jesus in our family.

No marriage or family is perfect, and we've had our times of struggle and suffering. In the darkest moments of our marriage, what helped us to keep on loving each other was having a relationship with Jesus, crucified and forsaken, who said he would take all of our sufferings onto himself.

The Focolare Movement brought us from one level to a completely different one. Even though it was a very difficult time, and we almost broke up, we can look back now and say 'Thank God that happened' and that we'd had a loving faith base.

None of us wants to suffer, but sufferings will hit us, no matter what we are doing or where we are. Because of our experiences, and because we have been able to live through those difficult moments together, we believe that suffering doesn't have to be a totally negative thing. It is something that, if we live it well, can be very positive. It helps us to grow, it brings us closer together and gives us a stronger relationship.

These days, everyone is looking for perfection in marriage. But, when things go wrong, we tend to give up too easily. With a strong spirituality, though, we can persevere, keep on going, and see it as a gift, as a way of maturing, of bringing us into an even greater love. It becomes

more perfect when you go through the crisis. We're not saying it was easy, but it was a way of not giving up.

One thing the Pope says is that love never gives up. God never gives up in loving us, so why should we give up on loving each other.

We are Sarah and Declan O'Brien, parents of five, most of whom live abroad. Our spare time involves lots of travel as we love spending time with our children, and, of course, with our four grandchildren.

We enjoyed our children as they grew up and tried our best to give them the experience of a loving family life and an understanding of God and his immense

love for us. We thank God that we have loving relationships with them all and with their own families. We continue this journey of love with them.

We were both on one of the World Meeting of Families 2018 panels during the Pastoral Congress in the RDS: 'Handing on the Faith between the Generations: The Role of Grandparents.'

We were also very privileged in our parish to lead the 'Parish Conversations' and to work with the children in the local primary school on 'One Hundred Thousand Acts of Kindness'; both helped us prepare for the World Meeting of Families 2018.

SALLYANN AND TORBJÖRN HUSS

We met in a shared student kitchen in Stockholm, while I was an Erasmus student. It was a lovely way for us to slowly get to know each other, and we both had an interest in cooking, which helped. I had heard about a Bible study group; it was something I'd never gone to before, and I don't know what gave me the idea to ask Torbjörn to that.

He initially said 'probably not.' He was a Lutheran from birth, but was 'searching' at the time, so he did come along in the end.

It's funny how life goes, how you can see the finger of God guiding your way. When I was in Sweden, the Bishop of Stockholm, Anders Arborelius, who is now the first Cardinal of Scandinavia, invited the students to meet him.

I went along on my own, and it was through this meeting that I heard about a group going to World Youth Day in Rome that year (2000).

On that trip, Bishop Arborelius had said to us all: 'This experience will change your life.' That was a big statement to make, so it stuck out in my mind. If it wasn't for World Youth Day, though, I wouldn't have gone to the International Eucharistic Congress in Dublin twelve years later.

When I heard about it, I thought: We have to go to this as a couple, even though I have no clue what it is and nobody I know is going to it. But, because I had been to World Youth Day, and people had travelled from all over the world to it and would be doing the same for the Eucharistic Congress, and this was right on our doorstep, something was pulling me to go.

We had been going through a difficult period in our marriage at that time. When we booked the tickets, things were okay, but by the time it came around that summer, things had really plummeted and we were really struggling. We barely even got there but it was really fortunate that we did.

We couldn't get into the first talk because it was full. So, we started wandering around in the congress centre, and came across a stand run by an organisation called Retrouvaille [a Catholic marriage-guidance programme]. That seemed like something we could do with, so we asked if they were giving a talk at the Eucharistic Congress and we were pointed up the stairs. We got in the back way to the talk and were the first ones in the room - if we'd gone in the proper way, we would never have got in because the queues were too long.

The talk consisted of three couples speaking about difficulties in their marriage and how Retrouvaille had helped them.

It wasn't just the women speaking, which is often the case in these things. We got the husbands' and the wives' perspectives on whatever difficulties there were. And they didn't go into a huge amount of detail but just hearing anyone speak about problems in their marriage was very unusual and refreshing for us, and it gave us hope for our own marriage.

Everything changed that day, it helped to open us up, and especially for Torbjörn to hear men expressing

how they felt about difficulties in their own marriages and how it had affected them. It was important for me as well to hear a man's perspective, because men never talk about those things. I could identify with what they were saying as well because that's what I was hearing from Torbjörn.

It was a life-transforming experience. It gave us hope that there was some solution out there for us - that we could work it out. It explained a lot of what we were experiencing and it gave us something to work on until we got on the Retrouvaille course later that year.

It's a Catholic programme, but it's not religious as such, although it has a spiritual dimension. One couple last year said it was the closest they'd ever been to God, sitting in that room with all of these couples trying to work on their marriages, being so honest with each other, and the forgiveness that takes place there.

The couples don't share with the group, they only share with their own spouses, which is also a benefit because a lot of couples feel ashamed at having problems in their marriages and they don't want to disclose them.

Most couples face a crisis at some point but, at the time, you feel like you're the only one going through it. It helps to be part of a group.

On that Friday evening of the weekend programme, you walk in and feel ashamed to be there, but by the Sunday you are transformed already – even though it's still only one part of the programme that has been completed.

That's what motivates us to volunteer as co-ordinators for Retrouvaille, because we realise how common it is to have problems in a marriage, how close we would have come to splitting up, how happy we are that we got help and how many couples need it.

We were giving our personal testimony at the National Eucharistic Congress in Knock in 2015 on the same day that the World Meeting of Families closed in Philadelphia, and the announcement was made that Dublin would be hosting the next one in 2018. The World Meeting of Families 2018 General Manager, Anne Griffin, pointed out the links to us; she could see how somebody was pulling the strings for us.

We are Sallyann and Torbjörn Huss and we participated in a panel discussion at the World Meeting of Families 2018 congress on the subject of 'Coping with Crisis in Marriage' – once you get the gift of healing in your marriage you want to pass it on; you don't want to keep it to yourself, because you are so grateful.

We are Shane and Leanne Hyland, both teachers from Sydney. We were selected as the Australian delegate family to attend the World Meeting of Families 2018 in Dublin with our three children, Joshua (12), Alyssa (8) and Lachlan (5).

It was a real honour and a wonderful opportunity for our family – we were delighted.

The kids were really excited to go overseas. It was great just to give them the opportunity to go somewhere and experience something bigger than our little church in Broken Bay. Joshua was looking forward to meeting the Pope!

Our youngest, Lachlan, had a very traumatic birth and, during his time in intensive care, we had a lot of people praying. He made a miraculous recovery, and doctors can't believe that he is functioning like a normal little boy.

It was God's love and it was the Holy Spirit. It was beautiful to see the life being brought back into him. Through sharing our stories with other families, we can make wonderful connections and find God's love in that.

Our faith is of great importance to us and we are passionate about supporting people on their journey of faith.

The World Meeting of Families 2018 was an amazing opportunity for us and our children to be with other families from around the world who are committed to living a life focused on Jesus Christ. We learned so much from them and look forward to sharing our experiences back here in our own parish and school, as well as in the wider Catholic community.

It's important for people to know that whatever situation they're in, the Church is there for them. And that, with their faith, there's hope in any situation.

THE HYLAND FAMILY

DARREN AND FIONA BUTLER

My brother died in a traffic accident when he was just eighteen, which had a huge effect on me. I had seen my mother's heart broken and the last thing I wanted to do was ever see that again. I was eleven at the time, but it was something that made me think twice about bringing any issues or troubles home.

Growing up in the inner city, I saw how Dublin was ravaged by drugs in the 1980s. I lost friends to drugs, but I think that luck played a certain part in the path I took and the people I met and with the friends I had, for whom sports were more important than drugs. Too many good mothers and fathers have lost children to think that it's just home life that puts someone on that pathway. Some young people experiment and don't see the dangers as much as others.

When I left school, I became an apprentice mechanic and then a printer. I fell into it, rather than looked for it. It served me well, but it wasn't what I really wanted to do, so I started to do some courses in the area of addiction and drugs. I became an advocate for young people in Co. Louth and from that to a job with the Irish Bishop's Drugs Initiative, which is based in Maynooth.

It's a problem that the Church saw had ravaged families and they felt they had to do something about it. We are a very small cog in a bigger wheel, but it is good to see the Church responding to these issues.

One of the aspects of my job is a peer-to-peer programme, organised through the Bishops' Conference and the HSE, in which transition year students are trained in a healthy lifestyle programme, and they then go on to facilitate a Confirmation class in their preparations.

Sometimes, with teenagers, the programme centres more on their beliefs and myths, because some think they know all about drugs – but they don't know the real facts.

For families today, the big issue is that risky behaviour these days is very different to what we would have got involved in years ago. Drugs are much

more widely available. There was a time when drugs wouldn't have reached certain parts of Ireland, but now there's not a parish or community that doesn't have the problem of drugs being available to young people.

Fiona and I met in a night club, Nightsbridge at the Arlington Hotel in Dublin, in 2002. We bought a house in Drogheda because we couldn't afford one in Dublin. We got married in 2005.

We went to Medjugorje together in 2004. It wasn't something that appealed to me at all – I'd lost my parents, and was struggling with my faith – but a group encouraged me to go and Fiona said she'd come with me. We got engaged there the following year. We brought loads of books with us, because we thought we'd be bored, that it would be all about praying. But we gave it a shot, and the week flew. When we came back, we felt the change.

That was a big part of my coming back to my faith. It was a fill-up, a renewal. And that would have been a big part of my now working for the Irish Bishops' Drugs Initiative – the main reason I went for that job was because reaching out and being able to help people in a pastoral way was a big opportunity, and it's been successful and rewarding.

I was involved in a workshop during the World Meeting of Families 2018 Pastoral Congress in the RDS. The talk was about addiction and the family. We had a number of speakers and testimony from those who've come through addiction. It's such a difficult subject, but the theme was hope, so people will come away from it seeing that there is a way out of addiction. We also had a silent drama performed by two people who have come through addiction in their family.

We are Darren and Fiona Butler, and we would like to think that every family in the country felt that Pope Francis was inviting all families, even those struggling with their faith, to come and see what we saw.

I'm originally from Co. Offaly, where I worked for Bord na Móna for four years, before moving to their head office in Pembroke Street in 1970. That's where I met my wife.

I was there for a couple of years and then moved to Cadbury's in Coolock. Apart from eating chocolate, I was in the engineering department and, as a senior project engineer, I was in charge of upgrading the factory.

This involved buying in machines from Switzerland, Italy, Germany or Holland, upgrading their designs to be more easy to clean and safe to work on and linking them in with our computer systems.

Growing up, Sunday Mass was the big thing. No matter hail, rain or snow, it took a lot to stop people from walking or cycling – there were very few cars in those early years – to the church.

It was frowned upon to miss Mass. Everyone knew everyone else and if you weren't there someone would be asking, 'Why wasn't Peter there? I wonder what's wrong.'

We went to see Pope John Paul II when he visited the Phoenix Park in 1979. Luckily for us, we came in through Whitegate and got into a corral very close to the Pope.

My biggest memory was the jumbo circling overhead.

My name is John Todd, and I was honoured to volunteer for the World Meeting of Families because I got such a kick out of the last Papal visit.

JOHN TODD

MARIA ROBINSON

I was in Galway for the Youth Mass with Pope John Paul II in 1979. The minibus driver warned us, before he let us out at the racecourse, not to hang around afterwards because he had to be back to Wexford in time to collect the women for bingo! I think we must have trimmed the hedges on the way home, we were going so fast.

I grew up in Enniscorthy with my parents and five siblings. Tragically, we lost our youngest brother, Peter, in a road accident when he was only nineteen. Our lives were turned upside down in a moment. It certainly taught me that life is for living and not to sweat the small stuff. I still think about Peter every day.

I think life was very straightforward then – I honestly don't remember the word 'stress' ever being used in relation to children or teens. My childhood was safe, secure and very ordinary – school, playing outdoors with all the children on the road, and Mass on Sunday in your good clothes and polished shoes! Just the same as everyone else. Once a year,

we were treated to a holiday by the sea on the Wexford coast. Even now, my husband and I love to go there with our own children.

I can clearly remember the annual Corpus Christi procession, when every corner of the route would have beautifully decorated archways and floral garlands across the streets, and the town literally came to a standstill. Every shop would clear out its window display and drape it with material, placing a picture or statue of the Sacred Heart along with a red glowing light or Our Lady surrounded by vases of flowers. Anyone who had a 'Papal flag' flew it from their upstairs window. The town looked fantastic and, as a small child, I thought it was the most beautiful place in the world – it didn't occur to me that other towns might be doing the same thing!

On Procession Sunday, we dressed in our best clothes. Women and girls wore either a white mantilla or a veil, and the men and boys wore a red sash. If you had made your First Communion or Confirmation that year, you got a chance to sport your beautiful dress or suit again! A lucky group of First Communion girls were chosen to carry baskets of rose petals to drop along the route ahead of the Blessed Sacrament – this was a great honour – and members of the Girl Guides or Boy Scouts marched along in uniform.

The local brass band was set up in the market square where the procession ended, and the town almost heaved with people. The weather always seemed to be sunny, and I can still hear my mother warning us to be careful not to stand or kneel in the tar on the road because it was melting in the heat, which would 'destroy our clothes'!

Our relations from outside the town came in to watch the procession, and it was a great opportunity to meet up with our cousins and our huge extended family!

I did my Leaving Cert in 1979 – the year Pope John Paul II visited Ireland. I got on a minibus at all hours on 30 September to head to the 'Youth

Mass' in Galway. We had a few hours of waiting before the Pope arrived – I spent it having a snooze against a bale of hay! It was a very memorable day. I'll never forget the cheering and clapping that seemed to go on and on after the Pope said: 'Young people of Ireland, I love you.' After we'd got our chance to wave to the Pope as he passed by in the popemobile, it was time to head back as quickly as possible to beat the traffic. I still have the ticket, which is proudly displayed behind my desk at work!

I spent a few months after that doing a 'commercial course' – learning to type and take shorthand notes. I landed one of those 'jobs for life' – permanent and pensionable, with good perks – in one of the major Irish banks, so I headed off to Dublin as a very eager seventeen-year-old. I thoroughly enjoyed my early working life and made so many friends, many of whom are still close to this day. After almost thirty-five years working in the one job, it was time for a change, and I enjoyed every minute of working for the World Meeting of Families 2018.

I met my husband, Rory, through Baldoyle Musical Society. I would highly recommend it as a great place to meet people – lasting relationships were forged there, and I'm happy to say that some of my close friends also met their other halves in the same place. We are twenty-six years married this December.

We now live in Swords and have two children, Olivia and Gary, both in their early twenties, along with two cats and a dog. Family is everything. We've had some fantastic times together over the years and we've made some very precious memories together. We do our own thing most of the time now but, like many other families, Christmas Day is our very special day together.

I'm very lucky to still have both of my parents, alive and well, at home in Enniscorthy. I visit regularly, as do my two sisters who live in Limerick. Two of my brothers still live at home – they didn't venture too far. We all pull together as a family to ensure our parents, who are in their late eighties, can continue to live safely in their own home.

My heart is still in Wexford, so if anyone asks where I'm from, I always start with, 'Well I'm from Wexford, but I'm living in Dublin a long time now.' A purple and gold flag will be flying outside my house yet again this summer in the hope that the 'Slaneysiders' might bring home the Liam McCarthy Cup. 'Dream on,' says my husband!

My name is Maria Robinson and I worked in the finance department of the World Meeting of Families 2018.

I have been a widower for the past year and a bit after losing my wife Anne.

I was at a Mass last July marking the first anniversary of my wife's passing. I spotted leaflets about the World Meeting of Families at the back of the church as I was leaving. I picked one up and read the call out for volunteers. I thought it would be a perfect opportunity for me to get involved in something new.

I think it was meant to be that I happened upon the leaflet on the first anniversary of Anne's death.

I think it was a great boost for Ireland that Pope Francis attended the World Meeting of Families. I think it will help people to refocus on the importance of family and faith.

My name is Paul Roche, and I volunteered for the World Meeting of Families 2018.

PAUL ROCHE

I thought it would be a perfect opportunity for me to get involved in something new.

EUGENE AND MARUSKA SMITH

We prayed for a year for a house, but thought we'd never afford one in Ireland. Then the prices started to drop and we went to see so many, but there was a point when we felt that it was not going to work out. We had been asking God to show us which one was the right house and one day we were on our way to Cork and got a phone call inviting us to a viewing the following week. We were sick of looking, but said we'd go along as we had been praying about it, and once we entered this house in Dublin, both of us felt very peaceful and knew that this was it.

When we were working overseas, we lived a life of providence. We weren't paid for what we did, but we had support and a roof over our heads. We learned to trust in God to provide for us. Even when we were getting married, we didn't have the money, but we trusted in God that he would provide.

We always had a great sense of trust in God's generosity. And both of us have a detachment from material things; even though we have a nice house, the most important things are our prayer life, our walk with God and our marriage together. They are the foundations of our life.

But, for a year, nothing was happening in our search for a house. We had to keep reminding ourselves that God was going to give us the right one; we wanted to believe that he had something prepared for us. Our prayer was: 'Lord, we give you this situation, you know what we need, we will leave it up to you.'

We wanted to do something for the Church, although we didn't know what – we weren't involved with Cana [ministry aimed at strengthening marriage and family] then – so we needed our house to be spacious enough. That was one of the criteria, and when we opened the door to this one, which was really spacious, we felt that this was the right thing.

We started going to Mass in an Augustinian retreat centre, five minutes from here. We had been struggling in our relationship, like every normal couple, but we needed to sort out

some things. After Mass one Sunday, a couple made a presentation. They had attended a one-week retreat for couples, called Cana, in England.

We looked at each other and said, 'Wow, we need that.' So, we decided that we'd participate in it that summer. There were six other couples from Ireland there too. There wasn't a lightning strike, but something dramatic happened in our relationship. There was a lot of forgiveness, a lot of opportunity for dialogue, to talk through difficulties and to discover ourselves.

At the time, Cana wasn't in Ireland, but we organised a monthly fraternity meeting with the other Irish couples who had attended. We wanted to set up a programme here, though. After two years of planning, the first Cana Ireland retreat took place in Athlone six years ago.

We were thrown in at the deep end, but we have noticed that every couple participating has a transformational experience in their relationship, because the Holy Spirit works very deeply during that week. Every July, we organise a

retreat for couples or families in Esker, Athenry, Co. Galway. There are events organised for children, which free up the couples to participate in the retreat.

The whole week is based around the wedding feast of Cana – it's looking at the old wine of your marriage, and asking Jesus to convert it into new wine. At the end of it, you hope that your marriage has experienced the new wine of Cana. There is a structure every day, but there is plenty of space for couples to go off and work on questions. In the afternoon, we have sharing groups. During the week, the grace flows from the Sacrament of Marriage, and you rediscover each other as a couple. You learn to pray together, to communicate and to forgive.

We met in Poland seventeen years ago, where we were both working on a Catholic mission. We got married in Prague in 2004, after which we were invited to set up a development programme on one of the dump sites in a Filipino city. We spent six months there working with a team of people on an educational programme for children, teaching them basic reading and writing skills, and there was also a vaccination programme and basic hygiene education.

Through prayer, we felt that God was calling us home. It was quite difficult stepping out of that working environment and to go and find work and re-invent ourselves. We moved in with Eugene's mother, because we were trying to get on our feet. It was a difficult time for us as we were not long married and we were trying to find our identity as a couple. We were struggling a lot.

Within the community we had been working in, there was a structure of prayer, so individually we were able to pray, but when we would try to pray as a married couple it was a disaster. Through Cana, though, we have learned to come together at least once per week to pray and to talk about our challenges and difficulties.

Cana is set up for people to experience, rather than to gain, knowledge, so it's a bit different to other retreats. It's not just the exercises we do as a couple, God is present as well. We invite God into our discussions. God is with us when we pray and we learn how to pray together as a couple.

We are Eugene and Maruska Smith and we were panellists for the 'When Plates Fly: Pope Francis on the Reality of Love in Family Life' discussion during the World Meeting of Families 2018 Pastoral Congress in the RDS in Dublin.

Even though we have a nice house, the most important things are our prayer life, our walk with God and our marriage together. They are the foundations of our life.

CAROLINE O'LEARY

I didn't know my mother was deaf, and I didn't realise that people could understand me quicker than her, until I was about five. I can remember being in a butcher's shop and my mam said to the guy behind the counter, 'Can I have three pork chops?' He looked fearful and went off to have a word with the other butcher, both looking at my mother. Mam was getting annoyed and told me to just tell the man, 'I want three pork chops.' I didn't understand and said, 'But you've told him already.' I did what I was told, though, and, as if by magic, the butcher understood me and three pork chops appeared. So that was when I realised: I understand Mam's voice, but others don't.

Both of my parents were deaf, and I'm the eldest of three, so the first people I ever met in my life were deaf and sign language was our first language.

Children of deaf adults (CODAs) have a great understanding of injustice and access in the world, and a sense of empathy and inclusion with anybody who is different. My mother became deaf at age six and my dad was discovered deaf at eighteen months. We three children and eleven grandchildren are all hearing.

When I was born in England, my grandparents sent my mam's sister, Frances, who was seventeen at the time, over to live with us, to help ensure I would learn how to talk! The public health nurse advised my mother that I had to go to playschool when I was two. It was a lot of unnecessary fuss as hearing children of deaf parents will always learn to talk because of contact with their 'hearing' extended family, television, radio, friends, neighbours and school.

My mam was educated in St Mary's School for Deaf Girls in Cabra, run by the Dominican Sisters, during which time there was a huge emphasis on oral education and speech. As a result, she spoke and signed to us, but Dad only signed, and when he would come home from work, the family all used Irish Sign Language (ISL).

I was born in Windsor, outside London, as my parents had left Ireland because

there were better job opportunities there for deaf people in the 1960s. Initially, they rented a television without sound but, when I was born, they paid extra for a television with sound for me to listen to. Marn used to put a radio in my pram. I asked how she knew if it was on the right frequency, and she said: 'A red light would come on.' I imagine I was probably listening to great music and chat with some crackling!

I have grown up pronouncing some words wrongly copied from my mother. I came to realise this from my friends and sometimes got embarrassed! Now I love all our mispronounced family words with much affection; it's a unique endearing experience shared amongst many CODAs the world over.

People can often be unintentionally patronising, asking can my parents drive, or can I read braille or if my home was really quiet – it wasn't! Deaf parents are noisy! My brother is a musician and he used to be up in his room jamming on his electric guitar late at night until our neighbours would come knocking on the door informing my parents to ask him to knock it off. There was never any policing of sound in our house! When I had my children, I was a noisy parent as well as I'd no experience of staying quiet so as not to wake the baby!

Another myth is that all deaf people can lip-read. The very best of the best lip-readers only get about 45 per cent of the conversation; some deaf people, on a one-to-one basis, conversing with someone they've become very familiar with, could get by. Lip-reading is not reliable to be able to get through situations like hospital appointments, though.

My parents didn't have access to our parent-teacher meetings growing up. They mostly went to deaf community events and we loved those occasions. It was then we saw our parents the same as everyone else's, if not leaders, and able to organise and participate at events. Then, contrasting that with where we lived, a lot of our neighbours thought that deaf people couldn't do much or they didn't get to know them. My mother, with another deaf woman, Alvean Jones, has just written a book, *Through the Arch*, a history of St Mary's School for Deaf Girls in Ireland over 170 years, and she was also one of the first 'signers' on *RTÉ News* and presented a deaf TV programme, *Sign of the Times*.

ISL is unique to Ireland. Originally, when deaf girls and boys were educated separately in Cabra, there were 'boy signs' and 'girl signs' as a result. When Irish deaf women would come together, they would sign away and use their 'girl signs', but when men joined in the conversation, boy signs became dominant in the conversation. A research PhD has been done on this phenomenon.

And in Northern Ireland, Protestant children learned British Sign Language, while Catholic children were sent to Dublin to receive a Catholic education and learned ISL. So, even now, when we meet deaf people in Northern Ireland, we can tell their religion; this is also unique to Ireland.

Things are better for deaf people than they were years ago. A lot depends on the deaf person themselves being proactive in saying 'I want this, and I'm not going to settle for anything less'. Last Christmas, the Irish Sign Language Act was enacted; deaf people now have a right to all public services with ISL interpretation provided. That was a thirty-year campaign. If a deaf person has to go to a hospital appointment, they request the hospital to book an interpreter; the hospital goes through an agency to do this.

There are still grey areas where it's not so easy to get an interpreter, like at parent-teacher meetings in a school. Or if a deaf parent wants to go to their hearing children's school play, a drama show, an exhibition, or an Irish dancing feis, it's an ongoing battle sometimes to constantly ask the school to provide interpreters, and it's difficult for deaf parents to get equal access.

My job with the Citizens Information Service is a really nice way to work with deaf people, because, when I work as an interpreter I am simply relaying the information, but I cannot advise, counsel or give my opinion. It can get a bit frustrating to see a deaf person not getting their needs met.

But in Citizens Information in the Deaf Village, we can assist deaf people from all over the country because they can call into the office, email, text, or Skype their queries. Somebody could be in Donegal and could show me a letter through Skype and I can sign back an explanation to them.

With so much that is telephone-based these days, it is a better world for deaf people, but there is still lots of room for improvement. We need more interpreters, there just aren't enough to meet the demand in Ireland.

Last year, the National Chaplaincy for Deaf People Ireland organised a nine-day pilgrimage to the Holy Land. There were sixty deaf people, twenty hearing people, three priests (Fr Gerard Tyrrell, who can use ISL; Fr Paddy Boyle and Fr Martin Noone), two chaplains, and five ISL interpreters. Together, we were able to give deaf people a fully-accessible pilgrimage. It was a truly wonderful experience for all of us.

My name is Caroline O'Leary, from Dublin. I'm a sign language interpreter and also work part time as an information/advocacy officer in the Citizens Information Service in the Deaf Village, Ireland in Cabra.

I signed up as a volunteer for the World Meeting of Families 2018 because I missed the Pope's visit in 1979. I had to have foot surgery, so I was in hospital in Crumlin. The following day, my dad came to pick me up and he brought me to the Phoenix Park. He carried me up to the altar, where Pope John Paul II had celebrated Mass just hours before. So as soon as I heard Pope Francis was coming, I was straight in to volunteer!

FATHER DAMIAN MCNEICE

My uncle Joe did amazing work for the homeless in Belfast through the Legion of Mary. I met up with him one evening in 1988, when I was up there on a summer scheme. I was setting up a game of snooker when he put his hands into his jacket pocket and pulled out a £5 note; he then proceeded to frantically search the rest of his jacket.

When I asked him what was the matter, had he lost something, he replied: 'I was coming out of St Paul's earlier and I met one of the sisters from the Family of Adoration. I thought I put a fiver into her hand asking for prayers for an intention, but I gave her a betting docket by mistake! And I don't think the horse even ran!'

We spent the next five minutes in stitches, imagining what the poor Sisters must have made of the betting slip, the cryptic message of 'Newmarket 2.30...' with the strange name of a racehorse. That was typical of my uncle Joe: renewing his soul at Mass, seeking the support of others, prayers and laughter always in the mix.

Growing up, there were seven of us in the family home on the Navan Road in Dublin 7. It was a close-knit and happy home. My parents gave us a lovely family upbringing with daily examples of faith lived as love, giving of itself for those in your care. And as my Godmother, my late aunt Eilish, used to repeat: 'Where would we be without the prayers?'

I have very strong memories of walking as a family from our parish to the Phoenix Park on Saturday, 29 September 1979, to see Pope John Paul II, across the dewy grass, surrounded by the early morning mist, just as the sun was rising.

Dad was in hospital at the time, after undergoing a heart operation. There were no buses running, so, after the Mass, my mum and my eldest brother walked the several miles to the hospital to visit him. Father Joe Kelly, one of our local curates, had brought along a pair of Rosary beads that Pope John Paul II had given him, so that my dad could bless himself with them. It was a lovely gesture.

Dad died suddenly in 1982, aged just forty-eight. Over the decades, our family has spread out to Donegal, Clontarf, Blanchardstown and France. My mother still lives in that same house, with the garden my father planted, and I get to see her at least once a week, most often for Sunday lunch! Phones and apps are crucial for keeping in touch with everyone.

My name is Fr Damian McNeice, and I am a team assistant priest in Our Lady Mother of Divine Grace Parish, Ballygall, Dublin 11.

I'm also Master of Ceremonies to Archbishop Diarmuid Martin, and I assist in the Diocesan Liturgy Resource Centre, based in Holy Cross College. So, Fr Joe and Fr Harry and the rest of the parish team don't see much of me in Ballygall, but they are very supportive and patient.

To me, prayer is constantly welcoming the peace of heart breathed upon us by Christ. Without it, I'm rudderless. Often, I start the day with 7.25 a.m. Mass in Ballygall, praying with sixty to seventy faithful souls, and that helps me to begin the day well, turning everything towards the one who is the way, the truth and the life.

What kept me going in the midst of the myriad of work to be done for the visit of Pope Francis in August was the depth of goodness and faithfulness in the people who were part of the World Meeting of Families 2018, both volunteers and participants, and those working on the events. I experienced that so much at the International Eucharistic Congress in Dublin in 2012, and I felt sustained by it again in August.

Family is the place where we learn the giving and receiving of love and forgiveness. As Brother Roger of Taizé once put it: the essence of the Gospel is to make life beautiful for those God entrusts to your care. So, the family as the lived essence of the Gospel is crucial to the life of the Church, where we are gathered in a family of families under one Father, where Christ calls us his mother, sister and brother. It's where we belong, where we return to and the place from where we can start again.

Anyone who has had an accident or illness will know that it certainly puts things into perspective and helps you realise the important things in life. About four years ago, I went skiing for the first time. During the first lesson, I went over the side of a nursery slope and down an eight- to ten-foot drop on the other side. I landed, full force, on the ice below, breaking my hip socket and smashing my pelvis.

I was incapacitated for six months after the accident. Once I was discharged from hospital, I had to go home so that my parents could take care of me. Being 'Miss Independent', I hadn't lived at home for almost fifteen years, but during my recovery I was so grateful that they were there for me. I suppose that's what family is about, being there in the tough times – no matter what.

Breakfast is a big thing in our house. My parents have a pub, so finding time together can be difficult, and we usually all end up working together on the busy nights.

JANE MELLETT

Growing up in Carlow, I lived with my parents, my brother, my grandmother, and my grandaunt. It seemed quite normal then to have three generations in the one household.

My granny used to say prayers with us when we were little and I suppose I learned all the Catholic prayers from her. She was a very devout and prayerful lady.

My faith is hugely important to me. I've always been involved in Church in some way, from volunteering in my local parish as a teenager, to now as a parish pastoral worker for the Dublin Archdiocese. I find myself always wanting more, whether it be more study, more retreats, or more space for spiritual practice. I studied theology at various levels, taught religious education for a while in the UK and trained as a spiritual director.

The big draw for me is towards Christian spirituality and the social justice teaching of the Church. I've had many experiences of working in India with the Salesians and this has had a huge impact on me in terms of seeing faith in action and finding meaning in one's life. It really opened my eyes and gave me such a positive experience of the Church as a global family.

In Ireland, too, I see the goodness that is all around and people drawing strength and hope from the Gospel message.

I think faith helps us discover who we truly are and to ignore that part of ourselves is not healthy. It's like Jesus says: 'I have come so that you may have life and live it to the full!' To me, the message of Jesus is as relevant for society today as it was two thousand years ago. Jesus challenged systems that oppressed people and his message of 'Love of God and neighbour' is as challenging and as valid today as it was then.

My name is Jane Mellett and I was the Project Co-ordinator for 'Care for our Common Home', which aimed to 'green' the World Meeting of Families 2018. It involved inviting everyone into a conversation about what is happening to our beautiful world and the threats our planet faces as a result of environmental destruction. Pope Francis has written to each of us about this and invites us all to reflect and think about how much we consume, how we use the Earth's resources and how we can better care for our beautiful world.

During the World Meeting of Families 2018, this project encouraged everyone, through prayer, discussion and action, to think deeply about the kind of world we will leave to the generations coming after us. This is one of the most challenging issues of our time and I was grateful for the opportunities the World Meeting of Families 2018 offered to explore this with participants.

On a personal side, my actions – in terms of what I consume, what I buy and how often I drive my car – connect into my relationship with the world and people in poorer countries who are bearing the brunt of climate change. In India, where I worked with disadvantaged children through the Salesians Voluntary Overseas Programme, you can see the impact that climate change is having on their environment – the lack of access to water is very serious, and these problems are getting worse.

The choices we make here are affecting the world, but sometimes we may not connect the two. Per capita, we are among the worst polluters in the world, but we have the resources to cope in this country when the weather goes wrong for us. Others don't. It's a whole question of justice. If your relationship with the Earth is a good one, it benefits you as a person.

I've started cycling to work. Getting to Drumcondra in the car was taking over an hour, and eighty minutes on the bus, so I decided that I had to start thinking more about the environment! Cycling is the fastest way to get here and is also a 'good eco story' – and you get fit in the process!

Everyone can make little changes. It doesn't matter how big or small they are, it all contributes to caring for our common home.

MARIE GRIFFIN

I was working in a designated 'disadvantaged school' when free university education was introduced in the mid-1990s and was part of that wave that saw students being the first in their whole housing estates to go to college. Nowadays, in that school, a huge proportion of students go on to third-level education.

In 2000, I went as a leader to World Youth Day to Rome with the Council of Catholic Youth Care. It was a very emotional journey, with a real sense of pilgrimage – we were sleeping on the floor of a school for a week! But I got a sense then of what pilgrimage was, and what it was for young people to see how those from other countries live their faith lives and how they do it in a spirit of complete and utter joy and ordinariness. It was very uplifting. Pope John Paul II came to the Mass outside Rome where there were 2.1 million people sleeping in the field. I saw young people crying with the excitement.

I am the CEO of CEIST (Catholic Education and Irish Schools Trust)

and late last year we held a number of meetings for principals. Somebody came to talk to us about the World Meeting of Families 2018 – mainly about the resources and the volunteering opportunities. One or two principals said: 'Wouldn't it be great to go as a CEIST family?' So we put it out there. We have a number of schools in Dublin City and, using the model I had seen in Rome, we thought we would offer students the opportunity to come up and volunteer, and stay in the schools.

We thought that if we got a few hundred that we'd run with that, but the response was overwhelming and in the end we had 1,500 volunteers. There was absolutely no difficulty in getting teachers to sign up too. Some had been teaching for thirty years and were really excited about being part of it.

We didn't even have to sell the idea to the students, we just had to tell them about it! They had heard their parents and teachers talking about the last time the Pope came to Ireland. It was such a wonderful event, none of us has ever forgotten it, and I think they wanted to be part of something like that.

It also gave them an opportunity to volunteer and to meet people from all over the world who were there. It was a real pilgrimage because they were sleeping on hard floors, they were walking long distances – but they were able for that. Not everything has to be about comfort and ease.

We have four host schools in Dublin – Beaumont, Lucan, Clondalkin, and Warrenmount – so we had to make arrangements to feed the students, have some sort of entertainment for them in the evenings and have some way of waking them up at 5 a.m. in the morning!

I met my husband, John, in UCD, where I was studying psychology. I was involved in a social action group and he was involved in a different one – volunteering has its benefits! He's a vet and, a year after we were married – we'd just had a baby – we went out to Pemba, an island off Tanzania, to work on a project to improve the quality of the local cattle. The island had neither running water nor electricity but we got on really well. My eldest son was there from the time he was about three months old to when he was three and a bit. We also had another child while we were there. They had a wonderful time and could speak and understand Swahili better than we could. They could never get lost, as they stuck out like a sore thumb because they were white!

The project was very basic in that it was trying to improve the quality of the cattle so that they would have a better milk yield to give more protein to the people. It involved giving in-calf heifers to a farmer who had showed a bit of initiative. He got a better-quality animal, and another one on the way, and they taught him how to feed the animal so that there would be a better milk yield. The programme worked so well that islanders are actually exporting milk now. A simple thing, but it had a huge impact.

CEIST consists of 107 voluntary Catholic second-level schools, about sixty thousand boys and girls, in every part of the country. Our schools belong to five religious congregations, but particularly the Mercy and the Presentation orders. We have no fee-paying schools, as they were all established in the seventeenth and eighteenth centuries for the children of the poor, to provide Catholic education to those who wouldn't receive it otherwise.

Our main emphasis in CEIST is to see in each child the image and likeness of Jesus Christ. We are not just there to provide the state curriculum and prepare children for exams, we have a responsibility to respond to their holistic education as well. We want to enable children to flourish in whatever way is appropriate for them. That's why it is very important that we have a full programme of extracurricular activities, so that whatever gifts they have can be developed.

It goes back to the parable of whatever talents you are given that you use them to the best of your ability. We would see religion as being part of everything we do. In all of our schools, no matter where you look, you have to see our Catholic ethos – in our admissions policy, in our special needs policy, in our relationships with our students. There is no point having a good Religious Education class if we don't engage the students, nourish them in the fullness of their capacity, if we don't subscribe to Catholic social justice issues, if we don't engage with the local parish or community, because these are all parts of what we do.

My name is Marie Griffin and I was a volunteer for the World Meeting of Families 2018.

We decided to volunteer as a host family on the off chance that the organising committee would think Rathvilly, Co. Carlow, could work. My husband, Dave, and I commute the forty-three miles to Dublin every day. We thought it would be nice to embrace the World of Meeting of Families 2018 in the wider country, specifically in our small village.

I attended the training course on hosting and brought back what I learned to my parish. We aimed to offer ten bedrooms, but were truly blessed by so many local volunteers coming forward and, by the last count, we had beds to sleep forty-one pilgrims. This far-exceeded even our most optimistic aspirations when this idea was first conceived.

I was born and raised here in Carlow and, having lived abroad for a number of years, I was luckily able to return here to raise our three sons. I met my husband, Dave, in Bermuda! When I finished my accounting exams and my training with PWC in Dublin, I was sent on a six-week secondment to the island to work on a specific project at the time. The night after I arrived, I went along to a Super Bowl party, hosted by two Canadians, Dave and Mark. Dave and I hit it off and soon after he asked me out. Twenty-five years later, we are still together!

Our sons are almost all grown up now – our oldest is working in Cork, our middle son just finished college and our youngest is just starting in college.

Family life today is very different to when I was growing up. My family were farmers and my mother was always at home, so we had that permanent stability, no matter what.

She and Dad always had great faith and a huge belief in the power and will of God.

As a farmer's wife, Mum insisted that the stock should be blessed with holy water. If there were deaths of animals, she would go out to the fields with the holy water and sprinkle it around. She also led us in the Rosary as children growing up, kneeling down on the kitchen chairs on a winter's evening. She certainly took her role of handing on the faith to her family very seriously

We have a strong Christian ethos in our home and never start a meal without a prayer of thanks. Meal times are a really important part of our family life, where we all sit around the kitchen table and catch up on each other's lives.

and I can only hope I am doing half the job she did.

Today, life seems to be so much busier. My husband and I both work in Dublin and we struggle to get the balance right between work and family life. However, we have always tried to prioritise our sons and to instil in them the importance of family and faith. We are not devout by any means, but we try our best. My husband is not Catholic but is a Christian, and we have a strong Christian ethos in our home and never start a meal without a prayer of thanks. Meal times are a really important part of our family life, where we all sit around the kitchen table and catch up on each other's lives. We have enjoyed many trips together, and we really enjoy reminiscing over the many stories and adventures we have had together. Invariably, we will end up in peals of laughter, and what is more therapeutic or bonding than a good belly laugh?

We live in the countryside and despite the fact that we are not farmers, sometimes it feels like we are. We are surrounded by fields, mountains and forests, so it is a natural habitat for all sorts of wildlife and domestic animals. We are the proud owners of nine hens, five cats and one dog. Wild deer roam the forest around us and it is such a treat to happen upon them when out walking early in the morning. We also see badgers, hedgehogs, squirrels, rabbits and the dreaded foxes. We even have buzzards, pheasants and, would you believe it, woodpeckers! We are truly blessed to have all this on our doorstep.

My name is Bríd Saruwatari and I decided to volunteer as I felt that the World Meeting of Families 2018 was a wonderful and unique opportunity for me to celebrate being Catholic. And, given that life is so busy, I felt that if I did not volunteer it would pass me by and I would really regret it. I also had many great memories of the Pope's visit in 1979, despite being very young at the time. The opportunity to potentially relive those memories again was something I could not allow to pass me by.

LINDA O'SULLIVAN

My grandmother is the strongest woman I know and has built her whole life around raising her family. She battled breast cancer many years ago, lost her husband in 2007 and, last year, lost her son John at the very young age of fifty-two, but still held our family together and kept us going.

She celebrated her eightieth birthday in March and, as my Uncle Liam said on the night, she is the 'glue of the family that keeps us all together'.

She has also been the biggest influence when it comes to my faith. From as far back as I can remember, she brought us to Mass every Sunday and always had a little shrine at home with all of her holy things. I still have a strong faith, and I credit that to her and to my mother for bringing me up in a traditional Irish Catholic family.

Sometimes people – young and old – are amazed that I have faith. Young people are often portrayed as if they don't have faith anymore, but I do. It is something I'm proud of as it's made me who I am today. It is even more important now that I have two children of my own. Family life can be quite busy, so prayer is essential in winding down and taking stock of what I'm most grateful for and praising God for what I have.

Earlier this year, my daughter made her First Holy Communion, which was a huge milestone for her and for our family. It was a rite of passage that we have got her to that stage and that she put hard work into her preparations, and for that we are most proud. Even through the aftermath of a snow storm she was determined to get to her 'Do This in Memory' Mass, walking by foot to the church so she wouldn't miss it!

I'm very involved in her school and am vice chair of the parents' association, which keeps me busy throughout the year. I'm also very involved in my own parish; I sit on the parish council, I'm one of the parish's child safeguarding representatives and I do a lot of work with the children of the parish.

Family life can be quite busy, so prayer is essential in winding down and taking stock of what I'm most grateful for and praising God for what I have.

My name is Linda O'Sullivan, and I was a volunteer for the World Meeting of Families 2018. I decided to volunteer as I have memories of seeing photos from the last Papal visit and asking my Mam what it was like. She told me some great stories of people walking all the way to the Phoenix Park and the amazing atmosphere on the day. I suppose I wanted 'in' on something that will go down in history, to be able to tell my children, or future grandchildren, that I was there.

Donna: We met at the International Eucharistic Congress in 2012, where we were both volunteering in two different capacities. He was there with St John Ambulance Ireland and I was with the eucharistic ministers and in the disability area because I'm an emergency first responder.

Just after the Mass in Croke Park, a woman took a bit of a turn and Éadhmonn and I were trying to get the stretcher into an ambulance. We were focused on the operation at hand but I couldn't help notice him all the same.

I got his name from a mutual friend and made contact through Facebook. When he looked at my profile pictures, he realised that we had met two or three years earlier.

I had been on duty with another organisation covering an event and he was there as a marshal when somebody got injured.

We were delighted to have a second chance to meet thanks to the Eucharistic Congress. But it came close to not happening for us.

I had been asked to volunteer and I wanted to give something back as I've had years of ill health myself. But, ten days before it started, I twisted my ankle. I didn't know if I'd be able to go. My faith is extremely important to me though and I believed that 'himself' above would look after me. A week later, I felt comfortable enough to do it, and I am so grateful I did.

I made some fantastic friends at the Eucharistic Congress, and the camaraderie was unbelievable. If it wasn't for the Eucharistic Congress we wouldn't be a couple. We just wouldn't have met. And that's another reason why we got involved with the World Meeting of Families. We both wanted to give something back.

Growing up, our faith was very strong, thankfully. We were brought up being told: 'If there is a problem, you turn to God; if there isn't a problem, you turn to God. God is your friend always, no matter what.' There were four of us in the family but, unfortunately, we have had a lot of illness, so religion has played a key part in all our lives. With all of my own past

health problems, I know I would not be here if it weren't for my faith.

For the last papal visit to Knock in 1979, my dad signed up as a steward and walked to Knock. My mum stayed behind working in our petrol garage – which was obviously very busy with all the crowds coming to see Pope John Paul II – while also minding my six-month-old sister. Her friend took my older two siblings to the Mass. Even today, they talk about the visit.

Éadhmonn: I am an only child, and the Catholic ethos was engrained into me at a very young age, along with a mad interest in Gaelic games!

I didn't know what I wanted to do in life. I've always wanted to be in a job where I'm helping people, and the right path was only made clear through chatting to a priest friend. I told him that I was thinking of the priesthood or joining the ambulance service. He put it to me: 'You're answering the Lord's call, but you're picking two very different ways. Either way, you will be the one to put your life on the line for someone, potentially. I will support you, whatever decision you decide to make.'

That was just before the Eucharistic Congress in 2012, and, even at that stage, I volunteered for it not knowing what to expect from a major religious event. I decided that it might be something worth going to, so I signed up with St John Ambulance Ireland. I'm glad I did. As well as giving me a wonderful faith-filled experience, it also gave me the chance to meet Donna!

Faith wise, my grandmother from Cabra had a very big influence on me. She would always say: 'No matter what happens in your life, always remember God spoke first.' Basically, if it is the Lord's will, it will happen, and if it's not, something else is meant to happen to you. Even on the day she was laid to rest that phrase was recited by the priest, to which he added: 'Although I'm not sure if he does anymore now that you're up there!' That was the way she was.

We are Donna and Éadhmonn Mac Suibhne, and we volunteered for the World Meeting of Families 2018.

At ten-strong, we were the largest family representing Birmingham's Archdiocese at the World Meeting of Families 2018 in Dublin.

We spent quite some time studying the pastoral programme to work out what we wanted to take part in, and there was a real sense of excitement building among the children!

Not alone was it a real honour to be involved in this pilgrimage, it was also something that we had never done before.

I went to see Pope John Paul II and Pope Benedict when they came to England, and they were significant life moments for me. Seeing Pope Francis in Dublin was exactly the same.

God called me to be a wife to David and mother to Lucy, Beth, Ruth, Samuel, Kate, Sarah, Jude and Nathaniel. I find family life very joyful, and we wre honoured to celebrate that in Dublin.

My name is Tina Hope from Worcester Deanery, and I was one of a hundred people from across our diocese, led by Archbishop Bernard, to travel to Dublin for the World Meeting of Families 2018.

THE HOPE FAMILY
(ARCHDIOCESE OF BIRMINGHAM)

KATIE WRIGHT
(ARCHDIOCESE OF BIRMINGHAM)

When I let the Lord become the centre of my life, I never realised the strength he would give me – I had to face three suicide attempts by my husband. At times, the Lord carried me and showed me how to get through and how to stay positive for Kory, our girls and even myself.

Through prayer, he listened to my heartache and my anguish. He wiped every tear, and spoke words of encouragement to my girls. He saved us and I have no doubt that he would do it again and again.

When I look back, I realise God has always been close, allowing me to meet my husband when I was fifteen. Our love grew and grew. So much so that we have married each other twice; the second time all the more amazing than the first because it was under the Lord's roof!

He blessed us with the birth of two daughters, Rosey (9) and Mollie (7); he has helped to heal pain, with the loss of my husband's mother when he was just twenty-two, along with the strains of relationship troubles.

When Rosey was just five and had not long started her new Catholic primary school, she asked me if I loved Jesus. I said I did and asked why did she want to know. She told me that, even though we can't see Jesus, we feel him in our hearts every day. Those words have never left me.

It had taken us six long years to conceive Rosey, and it was through this beautiful gift from God that I heard my calling to be a disciple. From that moment on we, as a family, found our faith. We were re-baptised and confirmed into the Catholic Church, and became part of a wonderful parish at the Sacred Heart Church in Tamworth, Staffordshire.

Kory and I became eucharistic ministers, and we give Communion to the sick and housebound in our community. Rosey serves as an altar server, and Mollie is preparing for her First Holy Communion next year.

Not long after I was re-baptised, I went to see my mother. We were chatting and drinking tea, as normal, when she said that she and my dad had something for me. They handed me a statue of Jesus. It had been my grandmother's, and my dad said she would have liked me to have it.

I was overwhelmed – I was thirty-one at that stage, but I had not seen the statue since my grandmother had died

twenty-six years earlier. My dad is not a religious man, but he knew that, of all his siblings, he was the one who had to hold onto the statue after his mother died. He told me that it would feel more at home in my house.

My name is Katie Wright, and my family represented Lichfield deanery, in the Archdiocese of Birmingham, at the World Meeting of Families 2018.

We were thrilled, overwhelmed, and super excited to go on our first pilgrimage together, and we felt honoured to be on this beautiful journey where we deepened our faith and were part of something amazing.

We were enthused to be able to meet other families, not only from our diocese but from all around the world, to share prayers, love, stories, ideas and friendship. But the Papal Mass ... It's not every day you get to celebrate Mass with Pope Francis – so that was epic!

NIALL MCELWAINE

One of my memories of taking the train back to school after Christmas was passing places like Claremorris and Kiltimagh in Co. Mayo and seeing the young people heading off to England. It still affects me, the memory of their parents saying goodbye to them on the platform. They were young lads and girls with few skills of any kind, who had left school at primary level with no great prospects, not knowing where they were going to end up.

I grew up in Fanad, the far north of Donegal – next stop the North Pole – a small, rural place, with no employment prospects at all. If you got an education, you might get into teaching, the civil service or the county council. But if you didn't, you got the boat to England or Scotland to look for work and prospects there.

The nearest secondary school was twenty-five miles away. We couldn't afford to pay for boarding, so the only chance for an education was to get a scholarship of some kind. I was lucky enough to get one to Coláiste Éinne in Salthill, Galway City, a preparatory college for teacher training. It was a four-year course; if you passed the Inter Cert and the Leaving Cert, you were guaranteed a place in the training college.

I was the fourth of eight boys; three of the others also got scholarships to secondary school. One brother got a scholarship to Coláiste Éinne as well, but had to leave in 1943 when the army took the school over as a hospital. I was among the first lot to come back to the school in 1946. One brother went potato picking in Scotland – that was really the pits.

I was two weeks into teacher training in St Patrick's, Drumcondra, when I got a letter to say I'd been awarded a Gaeltacht scholarship to University College Galway as a result of the Leaving Cert I'd done. I also got a letter from my father to say that if I felt like doing the degree, I should.

I'd already started the two-year teacher training course, which came with a guaranteed job, and pretty much

a job at home in Donegal. But, by going to the university, you really didn't know where you'd end up.

Education had been important in our house, particularly to my mother, as she and my father had left school at primary level. My mother went to America in 1920, she came back in 1925 and got married in 1926. That's one of the things I never found out: Did she have an arrangement with my father to come back and marry him? I don't think I ever thought of asking her. She was not educated in the formal sense, but was a great reader and was a bright person in many ways. We didn't have a radio in the early days, but when we did get one she listened a lot and was very well-up on world affairs.

At the time of the Vatican Council, when a lot of people her age wouldn't accept the changes at all, she took everything in her stride – she was in her mid-sixties at the time.

I worked in the vocational school in Portarlington, where I was the principal for thirty-two years. I took early retirement in 1988, and my intention was to continue work I'd been doing with the Catholic Peace Movement. But then a former colleague asked me to fill in for someone for just eleven weeks. I did it, and enjoyed it immensely. As a teaching principal, the administration part of the job started at 4 p.m., and we often had night classes, so you wouldn't get home until 10 p.m.

Then, I ended up teaching in Portlaoise Prison for a few years, mostly working with political prisoners.

One young guy's father had retired and handed over his farm to him, but he got caught up with things and was jailed for five years. The father had to come out of retirement to run the farm again. These types of prisoners didn't want bookkeeping towards a Junior Cert or a Leaving Cert. This guy in particular wanted a system that would keep track of his large farm, for transactions and records.

He'd said of himself that education hadn't been important to him, but then this thing with the farming came up and he got this idea of doing a computer course. We became friends and I remember saying goodbye to him one Friday as he was due to be released on the Saturday. He thanked me for all I'd done for him. But then the IRA bombed Canary Wharf in 1996 and the release dates for political prisoners were off. So, I came back in the following week and he was still there – he'd gotten another year. He just got on with it and we continued where we left off.

My name is Niall McElwaine, and I was a volunteer for the World Meeting of Families 2018.

We are delighted to share Niall's interesting story in his native tongue:

Ceann de na cuimhní atá agam ar an turas dhá lá ar ais go dtí an mheánscoil i ndiaidh saoire na Nollag i stáisiúin traenach ar nós Coillte Mách agus Clár Chloinne Mhuiris, daoine óga a fheiceáil ar a mbealach go Sasana.

Cuireann an chuimhne sin isteach orm go fóill, a dtuismitheoirí ag fágáil slán leo ar an ardán. Buachaillí agus cailíní óga a bhí iontu gan mórán scileanna de chineál ar bith i ndiaidh an scoil a fhágáil ag an bhun-leibhéal, gan mórán dóchais agus gan fhios acu cá gcríochnódh siad suas.

Rugadh agus tógadh i bhFhánid mé, i dtuaisceart Thír Chonaill – an Mol Thuaidh an chéad stad eile, áit bheag tuaithe gan seans ar bith oibre. Dá bhfuighfeá oideachas meánscoile b'fhéidir go n-éireódh leat post a fháil mar mhúinteoir nó sa Stát Sheirbhis nó sa Chomhairle Contae. Ach muna bhfuair tú oideachas den dara leibhéal thóg tú an bád go Sasana ag lorg oibre agus slí bheatha.

Bhí an mheánscoil ba ghoire cúig mhíle fichead míle ó bhaile. Ní thiocfadh linn táillí scoil chónaithe a íoc agus is é an t-aon seans a bhí ann oideachas meánscoile a fháil scoláíreacht de chineál éigin a fháil. Bhí an t-ádh ormsa go bhfuair mé scoláíreacht go Coláíste Éinde i mBóthar na Trá i nGaillimh, coláiste ullmhúcháin don mhúinteoireacht. Cúrsa ceithre bliana a bhí ann agus dá n-éireódh leat sa

Mheán-Teist agus san Ard-Teist bhí tú cinnte áit a fháil sa Choláiste Oiliúna do Mhúinteoirí Bunscoile.

Ba mise an ceathrú duine d'ochtar buachaillí. Fuair triúr eile den chlann scoláireachtaí meánscoile. Fuair dearthair amháin, Pádraig, scoláireacht go Coláiste Éinde freisin ach bhí ar an rang ar fad an coláiste a fhágáil i 1943 nuair a ghlac an t-arm seilbh ar an choláiste mar ospuidéal i rith an chogaidh. Ba é mo rangsa an chéad dream a tháinig ar ais go dtí an coláiste i ndiaidh an chogaidh. Chuaigh dearthair amháin go hAlbain ag piocadh phrátaí, obair a bhí an-deacair.

Bhí coicíos caite agam sa Choláiste Oiliúna, Coláiste Phádraig, Droim Chonrach, nuair a fuair mé litir ón Roinn Oideachais gur bronnadh scoláíreacht Ghaeltachta orm go Coláiste na hIolscoile, Gaillimh. Fuiar mé litir ó m'athair ag an am céanna ag rá gur cheart dom dul go dtí an ollscoil dá mba mhaith liom é sin a dhéanamh.

Bhí tús curtha agam leis an chúrsa dhá bhliain oiliúna mar mhúinteoir bunscoile le post beagnach cinnte ina dhiaidh agus seans maith post a fháil sa bhaile i dTir Chonaill ach ní bhéadh fhios agat cá mbéífeá ag deireadh an chúrsa ollscoile.

Bhí oideachas tábhachtach sa bhaile, go h-áirithe do mo mháthair, mar d'fhág si féin agus m'athair an scoil ag bun-leibhéal. Chuaigh mo mháthair go Meiriceá i 1920, tháinig sí ar ais i 1925 agus pósadh í i 1926. Sin rud nach bhfuair mé amach riamh: An raibh socrú déanta aici le m'athair go dtiocfadh sí abhaile lena phósadh? Ní doigh liom gur smaoinigh mé riamh an cheist sin a chur uirthi. Ni raibh oideachas faighte aici taobh amuigh den bhunscoil ach rinne sí cuid mhór léitheoireachta agus ba bhean éirimiúil í. Ní raibh raidio againn nuair a bhi muid óg ach nuair a fuair muid é d'éist sí leis go rialta agus bhí eolas maith aici ar chúrsaí reatha.

Nuair a thárla Comhairle na Vatacáine bhí sé deacair ag cuid mhór dá comhaoisigh glacadh leis na h-athraithe ach ghlac sí leo gan stró – bhí sí ins na seascaidí ag an am.

Chaith mé blianta fada ag obair sa Ghairmscoil i gCúil an tSúdaire i gContae Laoise, áit a raibh mé im Phríomh-Oide ar feadh 32 bhliain. D'éirigh mé as an mhúinteoireacht i 1988 agus bhi sé ar intinn agam leanacht ar aghaidh leis an obair a bhi ar siúl agam leis an Ghluaiseacht Idirnáisiúnta Caitliceach Síochána, Pax Christi. Ach ansin d'iarr comhghleacaí orm áit duine dá mhúinteoirí a thógáil ar feadh a haon seachtain déag seachtain. Rinne mé é agus bhain mé an taitneamh as. Mar phríomhoide gairmscoile a bhí ag múineadh is minic a thosaigh an obair riaracháín ag 4 i.n. agus nuair a bhi ranganna oíche ar siúl ní bhéinn sa bhaile go dtí 10 i.n.

Chaith mé roinnt blianta ansin ag múineadh i bPríosún Phortlaoise, ag obair den chuid is mó le príosúnaigh Phoblachtánacha. Bhí fear óg amháin sa rang a raibh feirm aige ach go raibh ar a athair aire a thabhairt don fheirm nuair a bhí seisean sa phriosún. Ní raibh suim ag cuid de na príosúnaigh sa Teastas Sóisearach nó san Ard-Teistiméireacht, an fear óg seo go h-áirithe, theastaigh córas cuntaisíochta uaidh le cuntas a choinneáil ar obair na feirme.

Dúirt se faoi féin nach raibh suim ar bith aige in oideachas ach ansin nuair a bhí sé ag smaoineamh ar obair na feirme tháinig sé ar an tuairim gur chóir dó cúrsa ríomhaireachta a dhéanamh. D'éiríomar cairdiúil le chéíle agus is cuimhin liom slán a fhágáil aige trathnóna Aoine amháin mar go raibh sé le scaoileadh saor ar an Satharn. Ghabh sé buíochas liom as an obair a rinne mé leis. Ach ansin thárla an buamáil ag Canary Wharf i Londain agus cuireadh siar scaoileadh saor na bpríosúnach. Nuair a chuaigh mé isteach sa phríosún arís an tseachtain dár gcionn bhí sé ansin go fóill agus bliain eile le caitheamh aige istigh. Lean sé ar agaidh leis an obair agus chuaigh na ranganna ar aghaidh mar ba ghnath.

Niall Mac Giolla Bháin is ainm dom, agus is oibrí deonach le Cruinniú Domhanda na dTeaghlach 2018 mé.

MARIAN O'MEARA

In April 2003, my ex-husband, Liam, was diagnosed with lung cancer and given six months to live. This came as a major blow to us, particularly for our three girls. A decision had to be made very quickly as to who would look after him and so my daughter, Pauline, and I took on the role. She took time out from her job to be his main carer. While it was a sad time, it was also very rewarding for all three of us, with a lot of emotional healing all round.

As a family, we felt that past hurts from the break-up were healed, and my daughters were thrilled that once again we were able to share some good times and stories of when we had been together – in fact, I felt we could have been again re-united as a couple.

When he was well enough, the five of us went out as a family for meals and long drives. We spent lovely times together and he was surrounded with a lot of love and prayer. While he hadn't before been a great Mass-goer, he insisted on been brought to Mass each Sunday. The love and prayer around him were never ending and he had found great peace; and I feel this helped in extending his short life.

Many times when we felt the end was near, he pulled through. The power of prayer was amazing and strengthened all of us to cope after Liam's death eight months later on New Year's Day, 2004. Doctors were surprised he had lived so long, considering the cancer had already spread to the liver, but we firmly believe it was love, care and prayer that did it. The biggest disappointment for Liam was that he wasn't going to see his first grandchild, who was due in June 2004.

We had another scare this year. Pauline was due her first baby on 1 April but had problems during the pregnancy. Two days after Christmas, she was admitted to the Coombe with complications. On the morning of 1 January – coincidently, her dad's anniversary – she had to have an emergency section to bring Samuel into the world three months early. He weighed just 1lb 13oz and was described by the doctors as a miracle baby. He didn't need any breathing apparatus or

oxygen, but remained in ICU for two months. The whole experience was nerve-racking for us, not to mention our major concern for Pauline's own health.

On 16 March, he finally came home and, thankfully, hasn't looked back. The support and prayers from family, friends and work colleagues was overwhelming and without this it would have been a longer road. He is so strong now, and a whopping twelve pounds!

I come from a Gaeltacht area in north Co. Mayo, where we were all fluent Irish speakers. When I was only a few days old, we moved to Baltinglass on the border of Wicklow and Kildare, and we had to learn to speak English!

We were reared on a small farm, where we all worked hard to help my father with everything from milking cows to making cocks of hay, while my mother cooked the dinners or did the washing. We loved every minute of it, and I often think back to those happy days. Both my parents have gone to their reward since the 1990s.

We were a very close-knit family and faith was important to us. We prayed the Rosary at 9 p.m. every night and if a neighbour visited they joined in. In 1973, I left home and moved to Wicklow Town, where I met my husband, Liam, through work. We got married and we had three beautiful daughters – Denise, now living in Wexford; Pauline, now living in Dublin; and Deirdre, who works in the Czech Republic.

Liam and I both had to work to pay the mortgage and provide for our girls. But, after ten years together, our marriage came to an end, which was difficult for both of us and especially for our daughters.

Rearing three children on my own was very hard, but I did the best I could. I tried to follow the footsteps of my parents by bringing the faith to my girls. In 2006, when my faith consisted of 'the usual ritual', Pauline invited us all on a week-long trip to Medjugorje. My response was: 'I can maybe do three days of praying, but that's about it.' That wasn't an option, so I had to think long and hard about it. However, I gave in and we all headed off as a family, not expecting too much. I was not 'feeling it' for the first few days but, by the fourth day, I felt the peace take over.

I'd heard a lot about the love of Jesus and about having a relationship with him, but I never quite understood it. As the days unfolded, I certainly understood a lot more. We went to Mass in a retirement home, which was run by nuns, and within a split second of receiving Communion I had the strangest feeling – it was like I was hit by lightning. I was overwhelmed with emotion and I couldn't stop crying. It was then those words came back to me: 'You will know it when it hits.' It took me twenty minutes or more to gather myself and, to this day, I will never forget the experience.

This is where my relationship with Jesus really began and I continue this journey every day. I also learned so much about the power of forgiveness. The whole experience changed both my prayer life and my personal life for the better. I thank God every day for the good and the bad things that happen

in my life, and completely understand that everything happens for a reason. I thank Pauline for the push and for her inspiration as our group leader in Medjugorje. She has since brought many others and has provided the groups with her music and singing. I listen to her CD most days on the drive home and this also helps to keep me connected with the those in charge of my life – Jesus and Mary.

I worked for the International Eucharistic Congress in 2012, which was a chance of a lifetime. I can safely say that, in my thirty years of working, this was most definitely the most rewarding of all. Little did I think that during my lifetime I would again be part of another amazing event such as the World Meeting of Families 2018 and to have the pleasure of again working with Anne Griffin, the general manager. I have met some beautiful colleagues through both events and I'm so thankful for this.

My name is Marian O'Meara, and I was an administrative assistant with the World Meeting of Families 2018.

FATHER COLIN ROTHERY

I'd never thought about becoming a priest until God started knocking hard on my door when I was about thirty and, eventually, I started listening. I've just celebrated nine years being a priest, and have found out that my granny always said I'd be one!

I've had the privilege of being there at some of the most joyful and painful times in the lives of so many families. I especially enjoy talking to couples about the spirituality of their own vocation or celebrating weddings and baptisms. At funerals, I do my best to bring comfort and the hope of seeing each other again.

I got a great foundation in the faith from my parents. We've always been a family where Christian values, such as doing our best, working hard, respecting everyone and trying to be kind and truthful, were in the background of our daily choices. Our weekly trip to Mass reinforced our faith together.

We grew up before the internet, mobile phones and twenty-four-hour media, so there was a lot more conversation at the family table, playing games together indoors or outdoors, going to the cinema or watching the same TV show as the whole country!

These days, when I'm with my mum, my three sisters and their seven children, we have a lot of laughs just catching up, sharing a cup of tea or a meal together. The home-made bread and cakes are sensational!

God chose to grow up in a family and live an ordinary life for thirty years – family has always been the place where we learn who God is and it's the only place we can learn to be human. And if we don't know who God is, or how to be human, society goes downhill pretty fast.

Faith is my rock, whatever the world throws at me. As a Christian (and a priest), the ideal would be that I do everything for God all day every day, whether I'm praying or not, but the reality rarely matches that. Starting again from zero is the best thing to do!

If I manage to get up early enough, I try to start each day with at least half

My name is Fr Colin Rothery, and I was the Dublin Archdiocesan representative in Rome for the World Meeting of Families 2018. I lived with the Irish Palatines at the Church of St Silvester, right in the heart of the city, near the Italian Parliament. It was like living on St Stephen's Green!

It felt wonderful to welcome families from across the globe to my home town of Dublin to celebrate the joy of the Gospel with Pope Francis at the World Meeting of Families 2018.

an hour with the Lord, where words are less important than what's going on between us in the deepest part of the heart. Mass is the high point of my daily prayer, and there's the breviary prayers that priests say at different point in the day, as well as a daily Rosary when I'm walking or driving. My best prayers are usually a word or two calling for urgent help or saying thanks during the more challenging or joyful moments of the day!

My best prayers are usually a word or two calling for urgent help or saying thanks during the more challenging or joyful moments of the day!

MARY ANNE STOKES

I met my husband in college but, soon after graduating, he had to return to his home country of Cyprus to do mandatory military service. It was tough to be separated for nearly a year and a half, especially since he wasn't allowed to have his phone while on duty and only had internet access when he went home once a week. Sometimes we wrote letters to each other though, which was kind of romantic!

But, when he finished his service, he was free to come to Ireland and make it his home, which he did. We subsequently married in a tiny Catholic church in the scenic town of Kyrenia, on the north coast of Cyprus – guests said it was like something out of the movie *Mamma Mia!*

It was a very special day for us, with many family members and friends joining us from Ireland and other parts of Europe. The two cultures blended well on the day and celebrations went on 'til late!

Mustafa and I live in Celbridge, Co. Kildare, with our little girl, Leah (18

months), and we are also expecting a baby in December. Our home life is very different to the one I grew up in with Mam and Dad in Westmeath. We make an effort to keep the two cultures at the heart of family life.

We enjoy Cypriot food – lots of barbeques – and we try to either visit or host Mustafa's family every summer. With them being so far away from us, we really value the time we get to spend with them. We know we are really fortunate to have so many ways to keep in touch and to be able to travel freely to see them.

With only my family to rely on for babysitting and to help with the many other challenges of family life, we have become more appreciative of the support they give us, especially the important role that grandparents play in the world of small children.

We enjoy the simple things like cooking at home and taking walks in nature. Our little girl really likes animals so we visit pet farms and Dublin Zoo whenever we can. We like to think that it is we who are introducing her to the wonders of nature, but it is often she who introduces us to the true wonder!

My faith has always been important to me. When I was seventeen, I got a summer job in the local hospital, where I was really struck by how important faith was to people who were ill and even dying. One of my jobs was to dust down bedside lockers and I knocked over many Rosary beads, crosses and little bottles of holy water during that time!

This experience inspired me to study theology and sociology at university. One of the highlights of my college years was being a pilgrim at World Youth Day in Toronto, Canada, in 2002. I made so many good friends from that experience and I think that the people I met along the journey were key to growing my faith and relationship with God.

With family life being so hectic at the moment, times of calm are valued. Every year we take a trip to Knock and have always found it to be a place of peace. I was delighted that Pope Francis visited Knock; hopefully it has inspired more Irish people to visit in the future.

My name is Mary Anne Stokes, and I was a volunteer for the World Meeting of Families 2018. I was inspired to get involved by the wonderful experience working as a staff member for the International Eucharistic Congress in 2012.

At ten years of age, I wrote an essay to say that I wanted to be a Holy Faith Sister – I had forgotten all about it until it was given back to me sixteen years later!

I had been an only girl in my family for fourteen years and I was very shy, so my mother signed me up for a club for girls on Saturday afternoons which was run by the Legion of Mary. We must have been asked to write about what we wanted to do when we grew up. I was in fourth class in school at the time and I loved the sister teaching me, who was always getting me to do jobs for her.

Fast forward to when I was about twenty-six or twenty-seven, I was at a prayer meeting with my mother. I was dressed in my religious habit, when a lady came up to me. I recognised her, she had been a 'sister-leader' in the Legion of Mary, and said she had something at home that I would be interested in. She had kept my letter for seventeen years. She said it was the only one she had kept and had often wondered if I'd joined the Holy Faith Order.

When she gave it to me, I couldn't believe that I had been able to articulate what I wanted to do with my life at the age of ten. The essay was subsequently read out later that year at my final profession in Celbridge!

I grew up in Artane and even as a child I felt drawn to something deeper, but I did not know what it was. I grew up in a very strong faith-filled home, although I thought it was the same for everyone else. I was particularly influenced by my mother. We were always great friends. She used to always say: 'Good comes out of everything, no matter how bad a situation is. God will never let you down.' That has become part of my spirituality and philosophy.

This trust came from my mother's own faith, but definitely also from her experience of pain and her own loss. Her first fiancé died jumping off the Forty Foot [an historic swimming area in Dublin Bay] just six weeks before they were to get married, and she lost

a baby boy, which also brought a lot of pain to our family.

When I was a teenager, I didn't focus too much on religious life. I enjoyed myself socially. However, it was always in the back of my mind that I would take this journey or that I would at least try it. I entered the Holy Faith Sisters when I was eighteen, just after I did my Leaving Cert. I probably wanted to see how it would go, while giving myself the option of leaving if things didn't work out.

My parents supported me in whatever I wanted to do, just as they supported my brothers and my sister in the choices they made. For me, there was a rightness about my vocation from the very start. But it was a big change for the family, as my brother, who was a year younger than me, joined the Navy the same week that I left home.

Looking back, I think my parents, especially my mother, made a huge sacrifice – I wasn't making one, I was following my dream. I opted for this life of not getting married, not having a family. But, it's not like you are giving it up; you never had it to give it up. It is a sacrifice for the parents, though.

I can still remember the tears in my mother's and father's eyes the day they brought me to the novitiate in Glasnevin. While I did settle down quickly into my life's new journey, we only got to see our parents every four to six weeks after that. And while I did get home for a week before being received as a novice, it was another five years before I could go home for a visit.

That must have been so hard for our families, but it was a long time ago and things are very different now. And I knew about that when I was signing up!

But when you really believe in where you are going, nothing holds you back on the journey to fulfilling what you feel is your life's call.

Music is very significant in my life. I began learning the piano when I was eight years old. Piano was taught in the convent by a wonderful sister, Mary Declan. My regular visits to the convent for music, and my familiarity with this environment as a child, also influenced me towards religious life.

As in my faith life, my parents encouraged my music journey and we had a lot of music in the house. My dad played accordion, while my mother's love for music was in her appreciation of it. Her grandmother (my great grandmother) had been an opera singer and taught music, so music is definitely in the genes.

While I have been involved in primary, second-level and third-level education (the latter in the area of chaplaincy), I now work in the area of faith and music ministry. I direct a number of choirs and am involved in the area of pastoral ministry with a number of groups. I have been composing liturgical music for many years. Through this, I endeavour to reflect a message of hope, which relates back to my mother's influence of faith and hope in my life.

I find music very therapeutic, both in the composing of it and in playing it. Even without words, it transcends so much. I'm always fascinated that I can walk into a room of musicians that I have never met before and we can all play together. Music unites. It transcends communication and words; it brings hearts together, and it can help heal people.

Some of my work is with the Hospitaller Order of Saint John of God. One area of my work is in music therapy at Suzanne House, working with children with a life-limiting conditions. It is a privilege to spend time with them.

For those who suffer with Alzheimer's Disease, familiar music is so therapeutic. When I play old familiar songs, it brings them back to special times in their lives, and that in itself is healing. Sometimes

I'd hear a song that my mother or father used to love and, while I'd feel sad for their loss, music brings me close to them.

Family means a lot to me. I remain close to my sister, to my brothers and to my extended family. One of the most painful times in our family life was the death of my late sister-in law Liz, who died eighteen years ago, at the age of thirty-nine. She and my brother had moved to London a number of years before that. Liz was a wonderful woman of love, kindness and faith. This was such a difficult time both for my brother and their five children. While they are all grown up now, I still play a significant role in their lives and in the lives of all my nieces and nephews.

My name is Sr Marie Dunne, and I was a member of the choir for the Papal Mass in the Phoenix Park on 26 August. It was an experience I enjoyed repeating, having done the same for the visit of the then Pope John Paul II to Ireland in 1979.

For me, there was a rightness about my vocation from the very start. But it was a big change for the family, as my brother, who was a year younger than me, joined the Navy the same week that I left home.

JOHNNY DONNELLY

For the first nine months of my relationship with Aisling, I was planning how I would propose to her. When we met, I was the drummer in the Saw Doctors and was travelling all of the time – relationships were never going to work. She was my best friend's sister and had moved home to Galway around the same time as I came back for a month's break.

I was never getting married, I was never having kids, but it's an amazing moment when you know – it's a bit like the faith that's in you: if you have a path to follow, you know that it's right.

I went on tour in America for nine weeks, and I spent that time deciding on the poetry I would use for the proposal. I organised that the postman would deliver a letter to her, and poetry clues brought her to a field down by Lough Corrib. The passageway of six fields to the lake was lit with candles. When she got to the brow of the hill there was another poem: 'To continue the path, be sure what you do. Because if the heart is unsure, it can be broken in two. One man is a husband, a woman a wife. From here on forever, is the rest of your life.' (In other words, don't come down to me if you're going to say no!) We ended up building a house on the same site!

We have four children, but our youngest, Harry, spent his first two years in ICU. He had a muscular problem that no one could figure out and he would just stop breathing. He was pronounced dead on a few occasions. Moments like that change your life: in an ambulance, stuck in traffic on the M50, and being told that your son has passed – that doesn't go away from you.

Faith, beliefs, all these things come into play because you realise how powerless you are. There are moments that you don't want to live through, and you start looking for a higher something or other to get you through.

I remember when Harry stopped breathing at home. We had the oxygen there, but we couldn't bring him back to life. Two ambulances were sent,

one from Castlebar and another from Galway, as they knew Harry and knew it was a life or death scenario. My wife went in the ambulance with him and they headed to Galway. I had to wait for someone to come and mind our three other children. Aisling rang me to say they had stopped in the nearest village and to get there as soon as possible. Panic stations, I knew, we'd been here before, and I knew – this is it. I drove the two miles to the village, but just as I got there I saw the ambulance take off in front of me.

We were told afterwards that they had stopped the ambulance because they were struggling to keep him alive and needed to work on him. I'll never forget the journey behind the ambulance to the hospital, I was booting it to keep up, because I knew it was serious. I was continuously saying: 'Please be okay. Please be okay.' Shouting it out, tears running down my face to the extent that it was hard to see. I was on my own, while twenty yards in front of me was my wife and my son in the ambulance. We had been there before, but moments like that change you, and you turn to something else, to whatever spirit or god you believe in. It changes you, and it changed my outlook on life.

Harry is eleven now, and he's the happiest child you'd ever meet.

I'm the middle of five children, born in Dublin, but because my dad was in the bank, instead of getting more money, he got transferred to a bigger branch. So, I lived in Mullingar until I was five and then we moved to Ballaghaderreen, Co. Roscommon. We were there at the time of the famous bank raid; my father was the manager at the time – gun-to-the-head type of thing. After that, the branch closed down and we moved to Roscommon Town as a family about five months after. It was difficult to leave Ballaghaderreen when I was thirteen because all of my friends were there and I remember it being quite traumatic.

In 1989, when the Saw Doctors took off, I moved to Galway, and I've been based here ever since.

My name is Johnny Donnelly from Arcana, the global event specialists. We were involved with the International Eucharistic Congress in 2012, so we have a background with how a big religious event like the World Meeting of Families 2018 works. Yes, at the end of the day, it is an event, but there are sensibilities involved that need to be adhered to.

It's not all rock 'n' roll, it's not all flashing lights and loud noises but, at the same time, you're trying to create reflective moments with highs and lows. You do that through programming, bringing people on a journey.

Logistically, if we have to take one band off and bring someone else on, it can take about fifteen to twenty minutes, so we use the screens or sounds to try and create something in between.

We try to bring the audience on a journey, but the word 'reflective' is what's in my head, so you want people to reflect on their lives, their families, where they are at now, and living the moment – that's what programming is all about.

Operationally, I never understand 'the moment' until it's all finished, because you're so ingrained in the event that you just want everything to be right. This time around we had an altar being built, carpets being produced, things being painted – there were so many variables but you just had to deal with the various deadlines.

What will happen, at some stage, is someone will say something about the World Meeting of Families 2018 and I'll say, 'I was involved in that', and I'll have a little moment for myself.

It's great that the faith is still alive and well. Everyone is going through tough times, but you can either turn for help or go in the opposite direction.

ARCHBISHOP EAMON MARTIN

When I was a child, every morning before we went out to school, my mother, as she combed and brushed our hair, prayed with us a simple version of the morning offering: 'O my God, I give to you all I think and say and do. All my work and happy play I will give to God today.'

I was too young at the time to realise that my mother was teaching us as a family to offer to God everything that happens to us each day. As I got older I became conscious of offering not just the happy moments, but also the 'prayers, works and sufferings' of each day, including the pains and disappointments that can often be part of normal family living.

I was delighted much later in life to discover that in another Martin Family – that of St Louis, St Zelie, St Thérèse and her sisters at Lisieux – the idea of giving and offering to God was taught and lived. St Thérèse herself used to pray:

Lord Jesus, I unite myself to your perpetual, unceasing, universal Sacrifice. I offer myself to you every day of my life and every moment of every day, according to your most holy and adorable Will. Since you have been the victim of my salvation, I wish to be the victim of your love. Accept my desire, take my offering, and graciously hear my prayer. Let me live for love of you; let me die for love of you; let my last heartbeat be an act of perfect love.

The idea of 'offering up', especially when we face difficulties or sufferings, is something that is deep down in the Catholic spiritual tradition and is well worth rediscovering.

We are gently invited as individuals and as families to take up our cross, to 'offer up' all those daily 'let-downs' and annoyances that can be so frustrating if you let them 'get in' at you and 'eat you up', but, when you let go of them and unite them with Christ's suffering, can instead become liberating and uplifting.

As part of our preparations for the World Meeting of Families 2018, I dedicated a newly installed Family Stations of the Cross in the grounds of St Patrick's Cathedral, Armagh. I invited families to come and do the Stations together as we continued our preparations for the World Meeting of Families 2018.

My name is Archbishop Eamon Martin and I am continuing to pray for all families and for Pope Francis as we move on from our international gathering of families in Dublin in August 2018.

As I got older I became conscious of offering not just the happy moments, but also the 'prayers, works and sufferings' of each day, including the pains and disappointments that can often be part of normal family living.

EPHREM FEELEY

I live in Ashbourne, Co. Meath, with my wife, Giovanna, and three children, Lucy (4), Finian (2) and Stella (1). Obviously, it is a very busy household!

I met my wife through music – we were young first year students in college and she asked me how to go about joining the college choir. A walk down Clonliffe Road ... and the rest is history! We've been involved in music ministry together for over twenty years now.

Growing up, my family were very much into faith: we went to Mass every Sunday, prayed as a family and attended all parish events. I suppose I had two choices, like every person my age: to either accept and embrace this faith that was handed on to me, or to reject it. I am glad that during my late teens and early twenties I explored and accepted it, studying theology and music in Mater Dei and going on to be a religion teacher, organist and composer.

Both Giovanna and I are church musicians, and, even though we are responsible for leading the music while we are at Mass, we still bring Lucy (who sings along) and I think she gets a good experience of liturgy and is comfortable in church and with the parish clergy. Occasionally we read stories from the Bible at home and we say a prayer or sing a hymn at bedtime.

Music is my primary hobby – I am in a very lucky and privileged position that my work is also very much my hobby! I enjoy playing the piano, although rarely nowadays get a chance to do decent practice. I write music and have also been fortunate enough to see a lot of my music published.

I'd love to pray more. As a musician and composer, I pray through music. I can be deeply moved by the text or music of a hymn, and I think that public, communal prayer through Sunday liturgy is most meaningful when there is a good quality of music and where people feel comfortable about lending their voices to the liturgical song. St Augustine said that 'those who sing, pray twice.' There is much singing and

Ephrem Feeley (centre) with his wife,
Giovanna (right), and Cardinal Kevin Farrell (left).

music-making in our household and also in Mercy Navan where I teach. This is enriching, calming and perhaps brings us closer to God and to each other.

I wrote my first decent piece of liturgical music when I was seventeen or eighteen and have been writing ever since. In 2016, in preparation for the World Meeting of Families 2018, there was a call for composers to write an official hymn. Three times I started; two sketches ended up in the bin and the third attempt I nearly didn't finish. It was this third setting – 'A Joy for All the Earth' – that I submitted, and, on Good Friday 2017 (literally on the way out to the 3 p.m. service), Fr Tim Bartlett, Secretary General of the World Meeting of Families 2018, rang to congratulate me on my hymn being chosen.

It's absolutely amazing and humbling to see how this hymn has taken off. Every so often I get an email from abroad, from places such as Pakistan, Nigeria and the US, from someone looking for a copy or for information on the piece. I recently came across a version with Hindi subtitles! It has really driven home how international the World Meeting of Families 2018 was, and how global our Church is.

At times, I am struck by how a hymn that I wrote has touched someone. A few years back, a musician friend introduced me to her five-year-old daughter. She asked the daughter to sing the lullaby that she sang each night; the daughter sang the refrain of one of my psalms. She is now a teenager, not surprisingly still singing, and sang in the video of 'A Joy for All the Earth'! On another occasion, a former student contacted me to let me know that she had undergone major surgery; she sang one of my pieces to herself on the entire car journey into hospital. She has made a full recovery, and she now directs her own workplace choir.

One of my strong memories of childhood is when my parents attended the Papal Mass with Pope John Paul II in the Phoenix Park in 1979. I was way too young to attend, so I was minded by a neighbour. I remember the excitement and that they spoke about it for months afterwards. They had a blue access sticker for the Mass on their Peugeot estate car for years after. They're still alive, thank God, and they were able to attend the World Meeting of Families 2018 Pastoral Congress in the RDS and the Festival of Families in Croke Park.

What I loved about the whole World Meeting of Families 2018 was the celebratory aspect of the Festival of Families on Saturday, and, of course, the Papal Mass with Pope Francis on the Sunday. In a time of upheaval in the Irish Church, it was wonderful to see so many people gathered in the Phoenix Park for the Closing Mass of the World Meeting of Families 2018 which included my composition.

My name is Ephrem Feeley, and I am the composer of the official hymn for the World Meeting of Families 2018.

FATHER LA FLYNN
(LOUGH DERG)

Growing up in a rural parish in the 1950s, it would have taken a lot of courage to stay away from Mass. Whereas now it takes courage for the younger generation to go to Mass. Even for adults, it's not unusual to hear stories of them being quizzed by friends: 'Surely, you're not still going?'

I don't believe that Lough Derg can be immune to what's going on in the rest of Irish society, where there is a marked decline in religious practice, particularly, but not only, in the Catholic Church. That's the short answer to the reason for declining numbers coming here.

And yet, for all of that, we'd be very conscious that while a proportion of the people who come here are faithful regular Sunday Mass-goers, we do get a significant number of people for whom Lough Derg may be the one time of the year when they connect with formal Church and the sacramental practice. Pilgrimage is an opt-in, rather than a requirement; people need to feel a freedom to come on pilgrimage, without an expectation and requirement that they have to sign up for everything.

When I first worked here in 1978, I was two years ordained, and I remember that year there were 16,500 pilgrims over the eleven weeks of the season. By the end of the 1980s, we had over twenty-nine thousand. One of the priests who'd worked here used to keep a keen tally on the numbers day-by-day, and he thought we might have hit thirty thousand that year. He was very disappointed when we fell short by a couple of hundred!

In the historical record, it is clear that the numbers have gone up and down considerably. Huge numbers came in the Famine and post-Famine period, but in the late 1880s they were down to three thousand in a season. Last year, we had about 5,500 on the three-day pilgrimage, and another 6,500 on one-day retreats in May and late August-September, which would have included some Confirmation groups and secondary school groups on retreats.

While the fabric of the island has

changed dramatically since I first came here as a secondary school student in 1968, the core of the pilgrimage exercises – the three-day fast, the twenty-four-hour vigil, the Station prayers on the penitential bed, the bare feet – hasn't changed. It's quite amazing to go back to the accounts of what happened when the first people came

here on pilgrimage to see that there is great continuity.

My colleague, Sharon, and I had the opportunity to represent Lough Derg at a gathering in Rome at the beginning of the Year of Mercy in January 2016. It was specifically for those engaged in the ministry of pilgrimage and retreat. There was an audience with the Holy

Father, and one of the things that has stayed with me so vividly from the short address was the ministry of welcome in places of pilgrimage.

Pope Francis is such a compassionate man, but he can speak so straight, and he was very challenging to those who are responsible for centres of pilgrimage. He said that everyone was to be welcomed as we would welcome Christ. And that we should avoid a superior attitude that may say: 'Ah sure, they're only spiritual tourists; holiday makers with a bit of religious thrown in.' Pope Francis was very keen that anyone who comes on pilgrimage would be given the presumption that they are on a journey, however explicitly or implicitly, and that they should be welcomed. Since this leadership role came to me last October, this has been something that I have tried to live with, and I do try to really be welcoming to everyone who comes my way.

My name is Fr La Flynn, and I am the Prior on Lough Derg, a place of Christian pilgrimage in the Diocese of Clogher since the fifth century. I'm originally from Rosslea, Co. Fermanagh, a border village in the southeast corner of the county, on a piece of land that juts into Co. Monaghan. Half of the parish is in Northern Ireland and half is in the Republic of Ireland, so what the implications of Brexit will be, who knows. My family had a pub but for as long as I can remember I was interested in being a priest. I've no memory of being called, because it was always there.

The World Meeting of Families 2018 was a great event for the Church in Ireland, and Pope Francis was very strategic in asking Ireland to take it on when it might have been held anywhere else. It captured my imagination and I can see the potential it has.

Our sense, in conversation with the permanent staff here, was that perhaps Lough Derg's particular contribution would be to support the World Meeting of Families 2018 in terms of prayer. Obviously, there was a huge amount of practical organisation needed to pull off an international event like this, but it was a spiritual event and, therefore, a key and unmistakable part of the preparation had to be the spiritual preparation of it.

We came up with the suggestion in 2017 that pilgrims on the three-day pilgrimage, who make nine station prayers in the course of their pilgrimage, would be invited to offer one of these station prayers for God to bless the World Meeting of Families 2018 with fruitfulness and spiritual success. When visitors got their pilgrim leaflet, they got an insert with an address label on it that they could peel off, sign and date to say they offered a Station prayer for the World Meeting of Families.

We created a pathway on boards, which looks like cobblestones, so people can stick their sticker on one of those spaces. Gradually, these cobblestones have filled up the pathway of prayer. That started last season and, with over five thousand station prayers and over three thousand this season, it was a significant prayer contribution.

Since this leadership role came to me last October, this has been something that I have tried to live with, and I do try to really be welcoming to everyone who comes my way.

SHARON HEARTY
(LOUGH DERG)

Dad was one of thirteen children, and his mum used to go away every year for three days. They often wondered where she went. Eventually, he asked her where she had been that caused her to come back so full of something that she didn't shout at them when they misbehaved! He then learned that she would go to Lough Derg, which she described as the holiday she needed every year!

I didn't know this story when I first came here with a bus load of others from Co. Down when I was just eighteen.

My dad took me to the bus in Newry and said, 'Do you really know where you're going?' I replied, 'Yeah, I've been in the Cathedral and I've read the poster.' I didn't really know where I was going, but I was doing my A-Levels at the time, and it was just something I wanted to do.

He didn't say any more, except that he'd pick me up from the bus afterwards and that we'd have a chat then. So, I went and did the pilgrimage and it was really hard. I'll never forget how hard it was; it was very wet that year and I wasn't really prepared.

I came with a group though and, when I look back now, we really did carry each other. I remember getting off the bus and into the car and Dad asked 'Well?' And I don't know why, but I replied, 'I'm going back there.' That certainly wasn't what I was thinking on the way home in the bus.

For me, Lough Derg is my spiritual home. Thirty years after that first visit, the prior got to know what I did for a living and happened to be interested in communications and outreach, so he asked me to come on board. I left the corporate and consultancy world behind and, for the first time ever, allowed my heart to guide me more than my head – and I haven't looked back since.

I love Lough Derg. It is challenging to market and communicate this island, but a privilege nonetheless. Even though it can be tough in the marketplace in schools and parishes with people saying they don't want to go because of the hardship, what fuels me every year are the people who have answered the call in their own hearts or the call that we have spread on our mission.

When you speak to them, you realise your work is worthwhile, because it's not about the numbers, it's about the experience – there are few places where you can walk away from everyday life and immerse yourself in an encounter like this.

Pilgrims come from all walks of life, and that's one of the things I love about this place – you can be someone who regularly goes to Mass or someone who is equally on the same journey over the three days, but who maybe hasn't gone into a church since the last time they were in Lough Derg.

Lough Derg has something very powerful, and I believe it is a privilege to communicate the message, because it has something for everyone, even though some may think isn't for them.

When you hear stories of people's first or fiftieth time coming here, you realise that there is a power in this place; that it

is giving something every year that they can get nowhere else.

Lough Derg dates back to the fifth century, as a place of pilgrimage known as Saints Island. The one behind it is Station Island, and that's where the earliest monastic settlements were. It was like the Google or Facebook of the time: a hive of activity, with people using their services, coming for vegetables, herbs, medicines and prayers.

So, the monks themselves needed to find a quiet place to stay, and they came to Station Island, the Sanctuary of St Patrick, also known through history as St Patrick's Purgatory. They'd come over to this island and pray in their beehive cells. People coming to Station Island would see the monks coming away to an even quieter place, and they wanted to be part of it. It has been a place of continuous pilgrimage down through the centuries, and the pilgrimage as you see it today, particularly the penitential prayer beds and the Station Prayers, come from that time.

It was closed many times throughout the centuries: through the Reformation and Penal Times, and when the island was plundered. But, even though the island was interrupted in terms of pilgrimage, people would still come to the lakeshore where the pier is on the mainland, and continued with their Station Prayers as best they could.

They were difficult times then, to get away to pray without being identified as having a faith. It can be challenging today as well. It's not easy to stand out in our own communities and say we have been to Lough Derg because it is so associated with being a place of faith. But this place continues to call

people. We are a resilient people and Lough Derg is a testament to that. It has stood the test of time and our faith will as well.

We wouldn't be here without the faith of pilgrims, whether they are pilgrims who are continually going and supporting the Church week-in-week-out or pilgrims who have a strong faith but are finding it difficult today. They come to Lough Derg to find their way back again.

My name is Sharon Hearty, and I've been the communications officer at Lough Derg for five years. We were involved in the preparations for the World Meeting of Families 2018 with our pilgrim way, through which we invited pilgrims to dedicate a Station Prayer to the preparation of the event.

We also took a stand at the World Meeting of Families 2018 Congress in the RDS and participated as best we could. We were delighted to be part of the preparations and to bring awareness of the event to our pilgrims in Lough Derg.

My paternal grandmother doesn't understand what it means to be a Catholic priest. She was one of my grandfather's two wives, and every time I go home she asks me if I've got married yet. I have to keep telling her that I'm a priest and I'm not allowed get married! She doesn't really understand, but she was the one who danced the most when I got ordained!

She's in her nineties now and takes care of her orphaned grandchildren. The life expectancy in Malawi is very short, between forty and fifty. I was saying to the people here on Lough Derg last night: 'I'm forty this year. I like coming back and forward to Ireland to replenish my life a little bit!'

I first came here about seven years ago when I was studying in Rome for a Master's Degree in Philosophy. I was looking for an English-speaking country to work in for the summer and I wrote to two bishops, one in Nottingham and the second was the bishop of Clogher. I got responses from both, but the latter rang me in person and said he had something for me to do.

I'd never been to a place like Lough Derg before; it's unique and very different from any other place. I took some pictures of the island and sent them home, but my family really have no idea what it is about. You need to be here to grasp the concept. Somebody can explain it, but you really need to experience it yourself. I've explained that it's a place of pilgrimage – that people come and pray, and walk barefoot – but they really cannot conceive what happens here.

There are four sons in my family. Neither of my parents grew up Catholic but, surprisingly, my mother has the strongest faith in the family. She was the one who encouraged us to go to church. I don't know where it came from, but she is extremely devout. The Church is her life, and she was so proud of me when I decided to join the priesthood.

We had a dictator in Malawi for over thirty years, and it was the Catholic

bishops and the Catholic Church that changed the fortunes of the people. People listened to the voice of the bishops, and it is still something that people respect in Malawi. The bishops hold some leverage, and when they say something, even against the government, the government listens.

I'm coming towards the end of my doctorate in NUI Galway and will be going back to Malawi immediately afterwards. I might be sent to a parish, but it all depends on my bishop. My diocese isn't too far away from some universities, so I hope to take a little bit of time out to teach for one or two days per week, so that whatever I have learned, I can impart that knowledge on others – especially on the youth; that's where my concern is.

If you don't help the youth, you might not have the Church that you want. You have to start talking to them and debating with them when they are younger so they can start to assimilate the role of the Church and what it does to change the lives of the people. In a country like Malawi, it's not just about prayer; it's actually the livelihood of the people that is affected by the impact of the Church. The Church is running schools and hospitals, so it has a big stake in the lives of the people.

I realised when I came to Ireland that Matthews is a surname. When I was a baby my parents were living in a rural place and, although they were not very Catholic then, they wanted me christened in the Catholic Church. They brought me to an out-church of their parish, to which a French priest had come to baptise hundreds of babies that day.

The time came for my parents to present me, and the priest asked what name they were giving their child. They replied: 'Alan'. But the priest said: 'No, you cannot baptise him with that name, he must have a Christian name. Choose another one.' My parents were at a loss; they weren't prepared for that. The catechist, a Malawian man, was beside them and he opened the Bible. He picked out the name Matthew, the first Evangelist. So this catechist, not knowing much English, recorded 'Matthews' as my name and it stuck. I still use Alan in some of my documents though!

My name is Fr Matthews Semba, and my bishop led a delegation from Malawi to the World Meeting of Families 2018.

My name is Nola. My mother chose the name. She wanted to call me Nola and had to give me the name Finola in order to get it shortened to Nola. I was still called Finola at school so nowadays if anyone calls me by that name I think I am back at school.

I have been to Lough Derg loads of times. I first came in 1981 and did it almost every year for about ten years. Then my kids arrived and I could not get the time to come while I was so busy with them. I have four wonderful children. As they got older I started back again at Lough Derg. I wasn't coming every year when I started back but I have done it a good few times now.

I always do the three-day pilgrimage; I have never done the one-day. My daughter has done the one-day – she came with a school and she liked it. She would not come on the three-day, however.

My twin sister has done the pilgrimage with me. There are just the two of us in our family. Her name is Geraldine but she's known as Gerry.

She came a couple of times because we had a special intention. The two of us were exhausted from the kids but we came and did it. We look very alike and everyone was watching the two of us propping each other up during the pilgrimage. We were trying to stay awake for most of the second day here on Lough Derg. That's what you do as sisters, as twins.

It's so wonderful to grow up with a twin. I didn't have any other brothers and sisters. It wasn't until after I was eighteen and had left school that I used the pronoun 'I' for the first time. Before that it was 'we' – we spoke as 'we' for the whole of our early lives. When we left school and went to college 'we' became 'I'. I did veterinary medicine and she did architecture – very different fields.

We are very different in that way – we are not identical – we do look very alike but we are not identical in other ways.

We don't have those twin moments where we feel things at the same time like some twins do but we never go a day without speaking to each other. She lives on one side of the country and I live on the other so we are separated geographically.

There is something unique about Lough Derg. I have a friend at work who is not Catholic and she came with me to Lough Derg to do the pilgrimage a few years ago. She had a very special intention for her daughter who was having difficulty having a baby and she came to pray for the special intention here on the island.

She did the three days. She had a chat with the priest and joined in the prayers. The weather was so awful those three days - it rained the whole time. It was a terrible first experience of Lough Derg for someone.

Her daughter went on to have four beautiful children and so both of them came back and did the one-day pilgrimage in thanks. That was very nice.

The island has changed a little bit down the years - or maybe the pilgrimage has changed. It feels a

little easier than it used to be. The dormitories are better; they are warmer and you have these lovely spaces to shelter inside just to take time out.

There used to be holes in some of the windows in the dorms or they would not close. I used to wear a hat in bed to keep the cold away. Doing the pilgrimage is penance but being that cold was a little bit over the top. Things are easier now.

Lough Derg is a place apart from the world and it always had this wonderful atmosphere – that has not changed. The prayers are so wonderful here.

The day I leave after the three days here I feel relief and I tell myself I am never coming back to do this again. But then you sort of get hooked on the pilgrimage and you just keep on coming back for some reason.

It's faith – of course it's faith – but I do the pilgrimage as a big prayer for all the things that I need and also now in my latter years I am becoming better at saying the thank yous, so I do it in thanksgiving too.

My name is Nola Leonard from Dunshaughlin. I am a pre-marriage facilitator in Accord and I was part of the stand for Accord at the World Meeing of Families 2018 Pastoral Congress in the RDS.

I missed the 1979 papal visit of Pope John Paul II as I was out of the country at the time. I feel bad that I missed it and that's why I definitely wanted to go this time, so I made sure to get in and book my tickets early!

I think Pope Francis is wonderful. He has a great pastoral approach with mercy at the heart of everything he does.

I was reading something by Fr Brian Grogan SJ the other day and in it he said 'How did we get from the love and the joy of God to the sick fear of the confessional?' That is the way it was. How did we do that? I think Pope Francis is trying to bring us back to the joy of God's love for us. I think it is so important that we would get back to talking and experiencing the joy of God's love for us.

There is a cycle to the pilgrimage on Lough Derg – as in life. Our lives are so busy that we fail to give it the focus it needs, unless we work through a transition into a quieter place. Lough Derg offers that opportunity, and people come back again and again for it.

The first day, when pilgrims complete the various Stations, tends to be very busy, but on the second day they are led to a place of quiet reflection.

After the busyness of that first day, and the vigil, they are led into a quieter day when they don't have as much to do. They only have one station, and spend their time reflecting and talking to people. As the waters recede and the normal distractions of life move away, a lot of issues – particularly with regard to the family – come up to the surface.

We need to create that transitional space in our own lives and create an environment in which God is valued and present. In some ways, that's what the World Meeting of Families 2018 did. While we do celebrate family life, to have a moment where we hold that in focus to really value it at the centre of the Church is so important. To take that moment and hold the family as the focus of what we're doing is to appreciate it even more.

FATHER EDDIE MCGEE
(LOUGH DERG)

We need to create that transitional space in our own lives and create an environment in which God is valued and present.

I come from Portaferry, at the end of the Ards Peninsula. There are seven of us in the family, three boys and four girls, like steps of stairs. They are all grown up and married with their own children now, so we've become a very large family.

As a priest, I've been very involved in family ministry for years. I work in Lisburn parish at the weekends, and I teach in St Mary's University, Belfast. For about thirteen years, I was involved with the youth team that went on pilgrimage to Lourdes. Then I got a call from the previous Lough Derg Prior, Fr Owen McEneaney, and he asked if I'd be available to work on the island. The dates were the same as when I'd be working in Lourdes, so I came to work here and have been doing so for the past five years.

My name is Fr Eddie McGee, and I am a priest in the Diocese of Down and Connor. I'm also the diocesan communications officer and was part of the team planning various events in the lead-up to the World Meeting of Families 2018. I was previously involved in the International Eucharistic Congress, so I was able to bring a bit of experience from that celebration in 2012 to the planning of the World Meeting of Families 2018.

Margaret: In our society, those of us who come to Lough Derg are definitely in the minority. On Lough Derg we are all similar. It's about us. Most people are doing it for someone or for some reason. One person I met is doing it out of thanks.

This was my third time on Lough Derg. I did it when I was in third year of secondary school, and then again in my Leaving Cert year, between the exams and the results. It worked! But then I didn't go at all until six years ago, and I have been going ever since. We all take the Friday off work to come up here for the three-day pilgrimage.

I think there used to be more people our own age and younger when I first started coming six or seven years ago.

I like that there's no media, no advertisements, no logos or signs; it's all just plain and natural and scenic. No one asks what you do for a living, but in real life it's one of the first questions asked.

When you're in the zone, you can do the pilgrimage; if you were told to do this in Dublin in your own life, you'd fall asleep – all you'd be thinking about is hunger. When you're in the environment, though, and you know this is what you have to do, you get on with it.

Edel: I have been to Lough Derg once previously, eleven years ago. I'm doing okay. Having friends with you is important, because they know if you are not acting as you usually would, that you're not doing so well.

Colleen: I come and pray for myself, and for other people. It's nice to get away from life, and you appreciate it so much after you leave the island.

We don't hand over our phones, but we make a conscious decision not to use them, and I turned my phone off for the weekend. It's one of the things I enjoy about coming here, you can totally switch off and have time with your own thoughts and prayers.

I first came here in 2008 with my mum, and we did it several times together until my mum had a hip and

knee operation and couldn't come anymore. So that's when my first cousin, Margaret, agreed to come with me.

I've never done it on my own, though you meet a lot of people who do. But it's nice to know that if you are struggling during the night, there is someone else with you. The night time vigil is the hardest, because you're tired and hungry, and you are walking around trying to keep your eyes open.

Everyone is on the same level and on the same page; we are all going through the same thing, and everyone talks to each other to help them through the night.

My name is Colleen from Donegal, and I attended the World Meeting of Families 2018 Papal Mass in the Phoenix Park with my mother.

BRENDA DRUMM

On 26 September 2007, my life was given back to me. It had been hovering for several months and we had been unable to plan for the future as a family. For those nine months there was a huge question mark where once the certainty of my life and future had been.

On 10 January 2007, I was diagnosed with incurable cancer. On receiving the diagnosis, I asked the question 'How long do I have to live?' I was told that they really couldn't say. Typical. Not only do I have cancer, I have a cancer that there is no cure for and now they are not even sure how long I am going to be around for! As a person who likes to plan and make lists, this was quite the challenge.

When I got over the shock – and believe it or not you do get over the shock of being told you are living with dying – I gradually opened my eyes and my ears and started to do research and to actively seek out other patients who have the same cancer so I could find out how long they had lived or were still living. I used to love meeting

someone who told me they were living with my cancer for five years. Mind you, as someone who is not that great at maths, I was constantly doing the maths and adding five years onto the ages of my kids so as I could work out how long I could potentially be around for them. Then I would meet someone who was living with my cancer for seven years and I did the maths again and added the seven to my kids' ages. Then I met someone who was ten years living with my cancer and I thought, 'that's better', but it still never felt like enough time for me and my family. I am still doing the maths, and this year I became one of those people that I looked for when I was first diagnosed as I mark twelve years of remission.

Any family living with serious illness will tell you that when a loved one is ill, it's the whole family that receives the diagnosis. I think the diagnosis is much harder for family and loved ones. They stand with you, watching you as you wrestle with the blackness of a diagnosis of cancer and then they have to watch, feeling helpless, as you go through the most awful treatment. They are the real unsung heroes in any cancer story. People tell me all the time that I am brave, but my heroes and the people who got me through my treatment are my family.

During my treatment, and many times since, I have thought about the wedding vows that my husband and I made with each other on 29 December 1995. Part of the vows included the words: 'I will stand by your side in good times and in bad, in sickness and in health.'

For so many years we had good times. Baby number one arrived in April 1997 and baby number two arrived in August 2004. Life was extraordinarily ordinary and we were blessed with good health.

When the diagnosis of cancer came in January 2007 I had to deliver the news to Bryan on the phone. He was in work but he dropped everything and made the journey to me. While telling him the awful news on the phone I had asked him not to be too nice to me when he arrived to the hospital as I needed not

to cry at that moment. When I think back I realise what an awful request that was. But I needed not to give in to the tears. I needed to feel I was in control. Bryan arrived to the hospital about forty minutes later and took me in his arms. Of course I cried and through my tears I said, 'I told you not to be too nice to me.'

All the way through the treatment he was there for me. He was wishing me well, willing me well. He took over all the 'mum jobs' I did at home without thinking and made sure all the chores were done. I somehow have ended up never having to lift an iron since I was diagnosed! Well, there have to be some perks!

I found some texts recently on an old mobile phone. They are from 2007 when I was in hospital at various times through that year (ten weeks in all):

10 January 2007 (day of diagnosis): 'Love u. Get a good night's sleep. Me and your mam will be up mid-morning. Bryan.'

14 July 2007 (mid-transplant): 'Feeling any better? Bryan.'

14 July 2007 (mid-transplant): 'You're almost there now. Just remember how much we all love you. Try to get some sleep. Bryan.'

I received texts like this every day from Bryan. He was faced with some terrible sights when he came to see me in the hospital as the side effects of the high-dose chemotherapy took hold. There were days I did not recognise myself when I looked in the mirror. Bryan never missed a day and always hid the shock he felt when he saw me.

He has more than fulfilled his side of the marriage vows in terms of the 'in sickness and in health' bit.

I know that serious illness and trauma can sometimes cause friction and fracture in a relationship and that some don't survive. As a family unit we have been through a lot, but we are strong, united and happy – even with this cloud of uncertainty above us.

There's a quote from F. Scott Fitzgerald which says: 'I fell in love with her courage, her sincerity, and her flaming self-respect. And it's these things I'd believe in ... I love her and it is the beginning of everything.' I am borrowing the last line from that and making it my own when I say: 'I love him and that is the beginning of everything.'

I have been blessed by my marriage and all it has brought into my life. I realise nowadays that this can be an exception and is therefore something to be cherished and valued. All I want for us now is to grow into an old married couple together and to be able to look back on this time of sickness as a small blip in a very big and wonderful life.

When we got the news in September 2007 that the transplant had worked we were so relieved. We could start to plan again. I could start to get back to life – literally. It still took about six months to recover fully from the physical effects of the transplant.

One of the major grieving moments for me after being diagnosed was the thought that there might be major moments in my kids' lives that I would miss should the worst happen.

World Meeting
of Families 2018

Cathal was only two when I was diagnosed and Emma was nine. I know some women who were diagnosed at the same time as I was who are sadly no longer here. That's the reality of this cancer. At times, I will stop in my tracks and think about those women. I remember speaking to one of them in particular. She had very young kids like me. She was busy before her treatment making recordings of herself reading her kids' favourite bedtime stories in her own voice so her kids would always have her voice when it was time for their bedtime story ... That's tough to think about. It's tough to have to plan for a time when your kids might no longer have their mum.

It's all so real and, at times, I feel the breath of serious illness on the back of my neck. I know my cancer will possibly come back. Even though the transplant was a success – there is no cure at the moment.

My son is now fourteen years old. He's handsome, funny and charming. He is into jokes, gaming and hanging out with his friends. He hates tidying his room and emptying the dishwasher! At the time of diagnosis, I was sure I would not see him even starting school, but I did. I am now looking forward to seeing him through secondary school and into college.

My daughter has just turned twenty-one and has blossomed into the most extraordinary young woman. She is beautiful, intelligent, funny and just brilliant. I thought I would miss her teenage years but I got to be here for all of that. I got to see her through her college degree which she finished this summer. I have been here to see her through so many milestones which we might have taken for granted before cancer.

I'm looking forward to new milestones with the kids – weddings, the grandkids – all the ordinary family milestones! We shared a wonderful milestone moment as a family in 2018 when we got to meet Pope Francis. We presented the official Icon of the World Meeting of Families 2018 to him with the Bushell family from Dublin. It was a blessing to do this as a family. It felt like a moment of great grace for us.

I want to be here for all the milestone moments – big and small – but I will be grateful to get whatever time I am given (twelve years and counting!).

I spent the whole of July 2007 as an in-patient in hospital as I received high-dose chemotherapy and a stem cell transplant. I was nursed in isolation and had a limited list of visitors due to the risk of infection to me. I did not leave my hospital room for the entire month.

If you had told me that twelve years later I would be involved in organising the World Meeting of Families 2018, the event that welcomed families from 116 countries, I would not have believed you. But there I was in the middle of it all.

I don't think I will ever get used to the fact that I might have to bow out of this one perfectly imperfect life a little earlier than I planned. Most days I try not to think about that and I focus on making memories and mischief with my family. My faith plays a big part in allowing me to live with this diagnosis. Faith is also what helped me through the darkest moments of my treatment. At times, so much of what I was feeling was difficult to verbalise and that's when my faith brought me through it.

I am still doing the maths! This past couple of years I was focused on the planning and the numbers associated with the World Meeting of Families 2018.

I am not one for doing a quote of the day but my motto for the last twelve years has been one I have borrowed from Jonathan Swift, who says it better than I ever could: 'May you live every day of your life.'

My name is Brenda Drumm, and I was Media and Communications Manager for the World Meeting of Families 2018.

GREG FROMHOLZ

I grew up in a broken family, with multiple divorces, and only brothers. So, having a daughter, as well as being part of a family with a mother and father at home together, has been a wonderful experience. I've been married to Alexandra for twenty-four years and we have three children, Chlöe, Joshua, and Eden, and a rambunctious puppy named Phoebe! Yes, it's hard work, but crafting life is.

Recently, our family has been feeling rattled. It was family stuff, work stuff, life stuff, a couple of sudden family deaths, and life transitions. We all have them, but the old demons of a peace-less and loveless fear reared their familiar heads.

Then, a friend showed up at our door with freshly-made enchiladas, as well as crisps, dips and ice-cream. It was simple – love often is – and enough to change our posture that day and that week. That afternoon, we saw a love that comes from heaven to earth; a love that tastes of enchiladas, that feels like the embrace of a family member or friend; a love that is the courage of forgiveness, and is found in the follow-through of living. It's all about the enchiladas. Sometimes, it's just that simple.

Family, in all of its guises, is a micro-society, a community that has an ability to love one another and extend that love beyond themselves, to be an overt manifestation of welcome. This is what Church can be, and should be.

Though I wrestle with my faith regularly, I have found it a sustaining wrestle in my life, a consistency of peace and turbulence. We have also encouraged our family to allow life and faith to collide and intertwine, to hunt for truth and justice, wherever it can be found.

Prayer in everyday life is important, but in one of those annoying, pebble-in-your-shoe ways – I miss that connection when I don't consciously and consistently make time for it, but I don't miss it enough to remember it every day. A bit like exercise and vegetables!

My name is Greg Fromholz, and I am an American living in Ireland for the past twenty-seven years. I was the co-ordinator for performers and artists at the World Meeting of Families 2018 Pastoral Congress in the family arena of the RDS, and the prelude and exit programmes for the Papal Mass in the Phoenix Park.

That afternoon, we saw a love that comes from heaven to earth; a love that tastes of enchiladas, that feels like the embrace of a family member or friend; a love that is the courage of forgiveness, and is found in the follow-through of living. It's all about the enchiladas. Sometimes, it's just that simple.

MARY KELLY

We were blessed with great parents. They had a very happy marriage, and our home was a place full of love and lots of music and singing. We were often known as the 'Von Trapps', as my mother played the piano and we had many great 'sing songs' down through the years!

I am the second eldest of seven. Growing up in Drumcondra, faith was hugely important to us as a family, and we went to Mass together, prayed regularly, went to May and October devotions and did the Novena of Grace to St Francis Xavier. I've been involved in the Church since about the age of ten, when I joined the local church choir.

As a teenager in the late sixties, I helped set up a folk group in the parish. Music has been a great gift in my life and, when my children were young, my sister and I took on the running of the children's choir in our parish for twenty years. Now we lead the singing at Mass every Sunday in St Brigid's, Blanchardstown.

I have been a member of a charismatic prayer group in our parish for over thirty years and this has led me into a deeper relationship with the Lord through the power of the Holy Spirit. Again, I am part of the music ministry of that prayer group and we meet weekly all year round.

I met my husband, Larry, back in 1976 when we were both leaders in two different youth clubs, through our involvement in the Catholic Youth Council. Our volunteering goes back a long way, and we continue to be actively involved in our parish.

We have two grown up daughters – one is married and living in Dublin, and the other is living and working in the Middle East.

Larry and I are part of a large group of volunteers who travel every September to Lourdes with the Dublin Diocesan Pilgrimage. It's always a very special time. We both volunteered for the World Meeting of Families 2018 – I was in the office once a week with the hosting section and Larry was a steward and minister of the Holy Communion.

My name is Mary Kelly, and Larry and I hosted a family of six from Croatia during the World Meeting of Families 2018.

When I first heard the request for host families, it immediately appealed to me. At an introductory meeting we were asked to become 'Host Visitors'. Larry and I visited many homes in our area to pass on information and prepare the paperwork. The parishes in our area came together to welcome pilgrims from Croatia, Zimbabwe, Spain and Argentina, and we were able to offer them some wonderful Irish hospitality and a 'Céad Míle Fáilte'.

CLAIRE DEVANEY

A few months ago, I was working in a parish with a large group of children for a Confirmation retreat when a fourth-class boy exclaimed: 'What about me? When will it be my turn to make my Confirmation?'

His words really struck me: what was being offered for him? Why should he have to wait two more years for his Church to offer to share in an engaging way the Gospel message? This young boy was hungry and ready to begin, on a deeper level, his journey of faith and what was there to give him?

From this encounter, an initiative called Catholic School Retreats was set up to help train parishes, dioceses and schools in how to engage more effectively in creative, vibrant and fun ministry for children.

Our children are important and they need to experience that they are wanted and that we are ready and equipped to bring the Gospel message to them in a way that is attractive, compelling and, above all, fun.

When it comes to working with children, we can sometimes feel unqualified or unskilled, or maybe we don't feel very confident in reaching out and engaging with them. But we have no need to fear. As St Don Bosco said, 'Make sure young people know they are loved, and they will follow you anywhere.'

Love and fun are the two key ingredients for children's ministry; if it is not fun, children usually aren't interested, and who doesn't need to have fun! And love, above all, is the most important factor. Children sense very quickly whether we truly care or not.

The family home is the first church children experience and so it is also really important that we help families to engage with their children in fun, faith-filled ways.

I have been working in children's ministry with lots of different churches and schools over the past few years, but working for the World Meeting of Families 2018 highlighted again for me how important it is to make room and to include and reach out to our younger members of the Church through creative, fun and innovative ways.

My name is Claire Devaney and I was the Children's Ministry Co-ordinator for the World Meeting of Families 2018.

The family home is the first church children experience and so it is also really important that we help families to engage with their children in fun, faith-filled ways.

NOEL KEATING

When I retired in 2012, after forty years as a teacher, principal and education officer, I felt called to promote the practice of meditation with children and young people. I had seen the practice being introduced to children in Australia and the UK, and I knew from my own daily practice of Christian meditation that meditation bears deep fruits in those who practise it regularly.

I visited the World Community for Christian Meditation in London in January 2012 and, with support from their outreach arm, Meditatio, and a team of interested teachers from Dublin, I launched the Meditation with Children Project that November.

Within a year, forty primary schools had adopted the whole-school practice of meditation – every child in every class within those primary schools meditated at least twice each week, all at the same time, with their teachers. And, to date, 160 schools have adopted the practice and over thirty-six thousand children have been introduced to the regular practice of meditation since 2013.

As co-ordinator of the project on behalf of Christian Meditation Ireland, I considered it a drawback that I had no formal qualification in spirituality, so I completed a Masters in Applied Christian Spirituality at All Hallows College, Dublin. For my thesis, I explored experiences of meditation of children from two schools. Research on adults has shown that meditation bears practical benefits, giving rise to improved physical, psychological, and emotional well-being.

The wisdom and religious traditions of the world have always asserted that meditation also gives rise to deep spiritual fruits. I was interested in investigating whether children enjoyed practical benefits and, more importantly, spiritual fruits from their whole-school practice. The results were very encouraging, and persuaded me to go on to undertake a PhD to explore the question further.

Over the next three years, I spoke with seventy children in four schools for an hour each. My analysis of the

parents to teach meditation to children. *Meditation with Children: A Resource for Teachers and Parents* was published in December 2017 and sold out quickly.

My name is Noel Keating, and I am National Co-ordinator for the Meditation with Children Project. We had an exhibition stand in the RDS during the World Meeting of Families 2018 Pastoral Congress. I also offered meditation workshops for young people in the Global Teen Village.

I come from a large family – I have eight brothers and one sister – and all ten of us are married now and have children of our own. We have always been a very close-knit family and we keep in touch very regularly through social media and, between christenings, milestone birthday celebrations and weddings, we manage to have a family gathering almost every year, often with all ten families together. I produce a family calendar every year with photos from significant family events from the past year across four generations.

conversations demonstrated that children do experience deep inner flourishing and spiritual fruits from their practice. Shortly after receiving my doctorate, Veritas agreed to publish a book to describe these findings in simple terms, and to help teachers and

FATHER CHRIS HAYDEN

Looking back, I marvel at how my parents communicated their own sense of faith without ever having harangued us – there is a lot to be said for quiet conviction and gentle regularity.

I am one of seven children, and my dear siblings have, over the years, presented me with no less than twenty-three nieces and nephews and one grand-niece! I have always felt blessed by being part of a large family. In addition to knocking corners off each other, my siblings and I make up a real network of support for each other and for our ageing parents.

Growing up, faith was central to our family life, but in a very gentle, understated, way. I never had any sense of being obliged to attend Mass any more than I felt obliged to eat my dinner or go on family holidays. Mass was simply part of the week – taken for granted, in the best sense of the phrase.

A crucial difference between today and forty or so years ago is that, now, faith is constantly challenged, constantly put on the back foot. This makes the task of parents much more difficult, as there are so many influences in their children's lives that direct them away from faith. There's no simple solution, but I think there are two keys needed to open the door of faith for children and young people.

We – parents, teachers, priests, and anyone else who is in a position to play a part – need to understand our faith better than ever, and we need to delight in it more than ever. If we can show that faith is both sensible and delightful, then we're moving in the right direction.

For me, family ministry tends to be woven into such activities as school chaplaincy and children's Masses. I love preaching to young children. Their engagement with the Gospel ranges from wisdom to hilarity. Parents tend to listen very carefully when their children are being addressed, and that can provide an opportunity for reaching adults also. Mind you, some of that parental concentration arises from concern over what a little theologian might come out with! Some time ago,

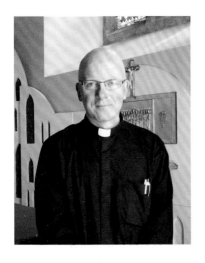

on the border of my home county of Wexford, and I also attend to the curacy of Shillelagh.

In addition to pastoral commitments, I am the editor of *Intercom* magazine, the Irish Bishops' monthly liturgical and pastoral resource. You could say that I wore two hats with regard to the World Meeting of Families 2018. Like everyone else, I looked forward to the event itself, and to the visit of Pope Francis. But I also followed things carefully with my editor's hat on!

after a discussion of the bread of life, a child told me, in front of her mother: 'We haven't had a proper breakfast yet!' Poor mother. But it was an early Mass!

God willing, the World Meeting of Families 2018 and the visit of Pope Francis has helped to renew our efforts. He has a gift for clarity, and he is a great witness to the joy of the Gospel.

My name is Fr Chris Hayden, and I am a priest of the Diocese of Ferns, based in the parish of Carnew. I live in Coolfancy,

A crucial difference between today and forty or so years ago is that, now, faith is constantly challenged, constantly put on the back foot.

I was eighteen years of age, and was not too religious, when I was first posted to the Lebanon; but, when you're out there, you do turn back to faith. I'd often say, 'Get me out of this, and I'll go to Mass the next week!'

At one stage, we were in a prefab and a 0.5, a heavy machine gun, took the top of the prefab off. We all ran for cover, and I was sheltering behind a tank stop, a concrete block, with a flare gun and a radio for seventy-two hours. It's in those times, you say: 'If I get out of this alive, I'll say a few extra prayers.' Unfortunately, we lost a couple of friends over there.

The Irish Army is regimental as well as religious, so that helped us get through it. And, for the six months you were abroad, you were probably more faithful than you'd be at home, and mindful of it. Faith is a big thing to every soldier, even though you might not talk about it, or shout about it.

Growing up in Drimnagh, we always went to Mass on a Sunday, but it was only in times when I needed my faith that I depended on it.

My father had been in the army before me; he did five years in the British Army and, in the late 1950s, he came back and joined the Irish Army. He served for twenty-one years and was still serving when I joined up in 1976. I was only sixteen then but in those days you could do that.

I met Antoinette in Ballyfermot three days before I went on that first trip overseas in 1980. A friend of mine introduced us. I met her on a Friday and shipped out to Lebanon on the Monday. For six months we were writing to each other. We got married a year after I came home and moved into a house in Clondalkin. We have three children: Charlene, Danielle, and Anthony.

I went back overseas to the Lebanon again for six months in 1990. I retired in 2007, after completing thirty-one years of service.

My name is Sgt Anthony Gallagher from the 2nd Field Artillery Regiment

Association, and I volunteered for the Papal Mass in the Phoenix Park. I was working with the army in 1979, when Pope John Paul II visited Ireland. We lined the route from Dublin Airport as he drove by – you felt as if he was looking at you as he drove by and waved.

A few months ago, I met with the volunteer manager, Richard Brennan, and he asked me, as chairman of the 2nd Field Artillery Regiment Association, if we would like to volunteer again. So, we had a meeting and I put it to the lads. We had twelve available who were more than happy to be part of it all.

ELIZABETH O'DONOGHUE

Hosting a family in our home during the World Meeting of Families 2018 was a way of reliving my own experience of childhood, where the door was always open.

I am the third of four children, and the only girl. Growing up in Galway in the 1980s and 1990s, we had a busy house with many visitors. Some just popped in for an afternoon, others for longer, but everyone was welcome and treated like family. I have only fond childhood memories growing up in Salthill, where there were strong links between the Church, school, and the community. Today, I think people are more guarded and slower to open their door to others.

Faith has played a significant part in my beliefs, and the wonder of God. I credit my parents for my faith, in particular my late father who, despite the weariness of illness, maintained his energy for prayer and participation in weekly Mass.

In 1984, for the close of the Marian year, we drove from Galway to Rome and back again in two weeks. A Tuam lady and her Italian husband had made all the bookings on our behalf. In preparation, my mother fed us pasta for weeks – a dish we only got once before as a starter!

I live in Rathfarnham with my husband, George, and our children, Joseph (10) and Sarah (8). We have visited Rome twice as a family. On the first visit, as Joseph was taking in the wonders of the Vatican, he declared he would like to serve for Pope Francis.

On our return in May, a parish worker in Arklow, Margaret Drew, made arrangements for us to visit the Irish Pontifical College. While there, Joseph served a Mass concelebrated by Fr Robert Smyth and Fr John Coughlan.

As a mother, I enjoy the role of my children in the Church and their many questions about God, heaven and their guardian angels.

Personally, I particularly like travelling and planning another adventure. We are all keen readers, with an interest in history. As a family, we enjoy walks with our dog, Teddy, and swimming.

I recently undertook a course in spirituality and mindfulness in Loreto House, Rathfarnham. I learned ways to bring quiet prayer into life, in both private and professional situations, and it gave me additional opportunities to pray.

My adoptive home of Rathfarnham has welcomed me into the fold with open arms. As the Jesus and Mary Order nurtured me and my family through school, the Loreto Sisters are feeding Sarah's spiritual and emotional growth. It is something I often thank God for.

My name is Elizabeth O'Donoghue, and my family welcomed an Ethiopian family into our home during the World Meeting of Families 2018.

Family, be they blood or selected, are, in my humble opinion, the key to wellness and being the best version of ourselves. It's where we learn loyalty, trust and kindness without need for reward.

My mum died when I was five, so I grew up without her. That impacted hugely on our family life. It has made me more aware, perhaps, of how important family is, how much it matters to me to be a mother to our children and how wonderful it is when we are together.

I grew up in Northern Ireland during the Troubles, which certainly impacted in every aspect of life. These days, I live in Letterkenny, Co. Donegal, with my husband of twenty-five years, Danny, and our four children. We have only one left at secondary school; two are at university in Dublin and one is working in Belfast.

Faith is central to my own life and to who we are as a family. We have always tried to pray with the children and to talk about faith. We believe that it is vital that the relationship with God is seen as part of everyday life, not something reserved for isolated 'holy moments' or an hour on Sunday. The challenge for Danny and I has been to bring our children up as people of faith in a society that so often perceives belief in God as something negative and retrograde.

Prayer has also always been important in my life. I remember as a very small child praying the Rosary with my mother and father and my brothers.

My name is Bairbre Cahill, and I was the moderator at 'Who is Doing the Dishes? Pope Francis on the Little Things that Matter in Family Life' during the World Meeting of Families 2018 Pastoral Congress in the RDS.

We believe that it is vital that the relationship with God is seen as part of everyday life, not something reserved for isolated 'holy moments' or an hour on Sunday. The challenge for Danny and I has been to bring our children up as people of faith in a society that so often perceives belief in God as something negative and retrograde.

SISTER KAREN KENT

Although not a Catholic, my father was very supportive of our being raised as Catholics. As children, when we questioned why he went to a different church, he changed his Sunday plans, went to the early morning Eucharist in the Church of England and then came to Mass with us later in the morning.

It was he who would read the Bible stories to us as children from a book given to the family by his own mother. This book is now in the possession of the next generation, who continue to enjoy the stories.

I grew up on the edge of a village in Staffordshire, England. My mother is from Wexford, and she met my father in Dublin when he was visiting from Cheshire. I recall, when we had no priest in our parish and the only available priest to cover the Sunday Masses was about thirty miles away, it was my father who would drive over early and bring a priest to our parish in time for 8 a.m. Mass. And then, having shared Sunday lunch with us, he would be driven back.

Faith was always part of our everyday life, and our family were very much part of the local parish community, so I grew up around Church and parish and a life rooted in Christ.

As children, my brother and I enjoyed two holidays each summer. The first with my mother's family in Ireland, where our days would revolve around the farm and milking and life was very relaxed. The second was with our other grandparents at their summer home in Wales. Life was more regimented and much more orderly than in Wexford, though, where it didn't matter as much if you were late in for dinner!

Today, I live in a large convent in Blackrock, Cork. Even though it was recently built, we have many empty rooms now as sisters have died and no one has joined us in Ireland since I entered the Ursulines in 1997.

Our community totals seven, with ages ranging from fifty-four to ninety-three. I am the youngest in my community by twenty years! During the year, we welcome sisters from around the world who come to improve their English or to experience life in another Ursuline Province for a few weeks.

Living in community is very different to growing up and living with a family. We are committed to a life of prayer and service, inspired by our foundress Sr Angela Merici, so it is very different to living with parents and siblings. In community, it is intergenerational living, with those you may not choose to live with, and it calls on us to make sacrifices and acknowledge our differences in so many ways.

Prayer is the centre of my daily life. I pray alone each day, sometimes in our chapel in the convent, sometimes in the church where I attend Mass each day or, on sunny days, I might pray in the Convent garden, and other days I pray in my room. But, as a community, we gather together each evening to pray Evening Prayer of the Church together before supper.

Family life is the bedrock of society and needs to be nourished and cared for as precious to us all.

Family life is the bedrock of society and needs to be nourished and cared for as precious to us all. I believe we all need to spend more time together, being family, eating together, sharing the story of family together, talking to each other, and sharing everyday activities together.

My name is Sr Karen Kent, and I am the vocations director for the Ursuline Province, so I give some time to promoting vocations, and attending events to spread the message about St Angela, and our way of life.

As co-ordinator of pastoral development in the Diocese of Cork and Ross, I was one of the delegates preparing for the World Meeting of Families 2018. So, I developed our own preparation programme for our parishes, which invited parishes to celebrate one event, either a feast day or a special time each month for the past year, and to record it on a parish calendar.

It was wonderful to hear all the international speakers at the Pastoral Congress in the RDS, to hear how other countries reach into families to support them.

Three months of piano lessons cost the same as half my father's weekly wages – vital funds from a family budget – but never once did he complain. He always produced the money willingly, anxious to give me whatever opportunities he could.

He was a devoted father and worked endlessly for all of his children, putting many of us through further education to ensure a better life for us. The selfless devotion of my parents to their children was surely love in its highest form and an example of the best of parenting.

I was born in Co. Fermanagh, to Mollie and Charlie McCarron, who were from neighbouring farming families in Tedd, Irvinestown. As a young man, my father left Ireland and travelled to find work in Scotland, where he was employed as the foreman – the 'gaffer' – laying pipes and installing water systems along roads all over the country. My mother also travelled to Scotland, where she worked as a cook in the classic 'big house'. They married and had a large family of thirteen children!

My father was a hard worker and a very intelligent man but, like many of his day, he didn't have the opportunity of an education beyond the age of fifteen. My mother was a refined and gentle lady. She was extremely creative and often to be found in the kitchen, turning out some delicious concoction she had dreamed up! She was the most patient of all mothers: strict, with great principles, but never once raising her voice to us!

Growing up, we were a very devout Catholic family, faithful Mass-goers and said the Rosary as a family ritual every night, kneeling by the chairs in our sitting room.

We were also musical, and all very good singers, but when I was thirteen, we bought a piano for five pounds, and it changed my life. I had never played a piano before but, from the moment it arrived, I strangely already knew how to play it! By week's end, I had a repertoire of hymns and pieces, much to the delight of my dear mother.

When I was sixteen, I applied and won a scholarship to the Royal Scottish

VERONICA McCARRON

Secondary School in Kilkenny. I started with fifty students in the Presentation choral programme, which grew to over three hundred.

Over the following twenty-two years, we entered many of the top choral festivals and competitions in the country, winning every major prize, some on several occasions. In 2016, we reached the live finals of *Britain's Got Talent*! After that, I retired from the school and formed ARÍS, a choir of vocally gifted and dedicated young women, most of whom were my RIAM voice students in the previous twenty years.

Since formation, we have performed at many prestigious events, including the World Irish Dancing Conference, the *Late Late Show*, the Daniel O'Donnell Christmas Gala Concert, the Pendulum Summit Conference and the recent opening ceremony of the Allianz Para Games at the Aquatic Centre in Dublin. We have also been extremely fortunate to receive the sponsorship of Allianz Insurance Company.

Academy of Music in Glasgow. I continued as a full-time student after high school, studying voice, piano and viola. I graduated in 1972, married, and had two children, Rory and Antony. I also embarked on my music career, teaching classroom and choral music all around the world for the next twenty-three years.

In 1995, I returned to Ireland, where I took up a position at the Presentation

In recent months, I have also taken on a new choral challenge, the Donegal 'Choir of Ages', a project by Donegal County Council's Department of Social Inclusion. We have over one hundred members, including children from the ages of seven to twelve, and adults from sixty-five to ninety!

While my life has been blessed with a loyal and loving family, good friends and a fulfilling musical career, I have also experienced tremendous sadness. My twenty-five-year marriage broke up in 1996. Having been raised as a strong Catholic, it was devastating for me.

A few years after this, I lost my beloved sister, father, brother and mother, all over a period of two years. But, worse was to come. In 2002, my beautiful son, Antony, who was twenty-seven, was killed in an accident in the USA, where he was working as a tree surgeon. He remained in a coma for several months, before finally passing away in January 2003. We brought him home to Ireland for burial.

I feel Antony is in heaven and orchestrating the many incredible experiences I have had since his death. He will always be close to Rory and I, as we travel our journey of life.

Through these events and tragedies, I have been sustained by a deep sense of faith in God, in my strong belief in life after death, in the goodness and kindness of people, by my love of music and my choral students and, most importantly, by my wonderful family – my son, Rory; my granddaughter, Eva; and my dearest sisters, brothers, nieces and nephews. I can truly say I am blessed!

My name is Veronica McCarron, and I am the choral director of ARÍS Celebration Choir, who performed for Pope Francis at the Festival of Families in Croke Park on Saturday 25 August. From the moment we learned of the Papal visit, I hoped and prayed that we in ARÍS would be invited to participate.

FATHER DERMOD MCCARTHY

The priesthood was always at the back of my mind, but I hadn't intended to become one. I was looking towards engineering actually, but a number of things happened that pointed me towards thinking about the priesthood again.

I was visiting the University Church, which I'd never been to before, with a classmate of mine, and happened to notice that there was a priest hearing confessions. There was a man sitting outside the box, who seemed quite upset, he looked very worried and nervous.

He then went into the confessional and we went to admire the mosaics around the church. As we were leaving, I happened to notice the man coming out of the box. He was like a different person. I thought to myself that whatever happened in that box was worth it to him, and that stuck with me.

I can still see him to this day. Whatever worry was on him was gone, he walked with a lighter step, as if he'd been greatly relieved of something.

So, I thought I'd give it a shot, and I came to the seminary at Holy Cross College in Drumcondra. My uncle was a priest here in Dublin, and I was no good at football – it seemed to me that you couldn't be a priest in Kilmore Diocese, where I was from, if you didn't know something about football! All the priests I knew were involved in GAA! So, I came to Dublin and have never looked back.

I was very into plays, directing them, lighting them and doing the sound. I was encouraged to develop that talent, and it led to being involved with the Radharc Films series of TV programmes afterwards from 1965, so I have to thank Holy Cross College for my broadcasting work.

People thought it was ground-breaking. It involved going to different parts of Ireland and the world making programmes about the Church and interesting people working in the Church. But it wasn't just doctrinal all of the time, we were dealing with the Biafra War and the famine in Biafra. We also did a programme about Rose

Kennedy, on the tenth anniversary of John F. Kennedy's death.

Radharc Films did over four hundred documentaries between 1962 and 1996 and filmed programmes in seventy-five countries. Missionaries were our researchers, our drivers and our stars! I like to think that the Brazil series, which we did in 1977, opened people's eyes in Ireland to a different form of Church.

A critic, Tom O'Dea, who used to write for the *Irish Press*, said: 'I couldn't help but feel that Radharc was making programmes about Brazil, but really looking through them to see the reality of life in Ireland underneath.'

That was true. Brazil was a much more people-orientated Church than the one we had here. I asked the Archbishop of São Paolo how many priests were involved in the running of the diocese – it stretched about forty miles across the city, and had a population of twenty million. He thought about it, as he puffed on his pipe, and said 'Hmmm, there are two priests involved in the administration of the diocese'. Everyone else was a lay person!

I could see by this that the Irish Church had to change, and it has changed for the better. It's still a bit too hierarchical, but is moving in the right direction, and this event, focused on families, has helped us to realise that lay people will have to carry it.

Some people are a bit despairing and down about the fact that priests are very few on the ground, but you'd wonder what was going through the mind of the monk who turned the key in the lock of Glendalough Abbey for the last time in the fifteenth century. He must have thought it was all finished, but a new Church came afterwards.

In 1991, RTÉ asked if I'd be interested in becoming head of religious programmes. I retired from that ten years ago, and was then asked by the director general if I'd take on a pastoral role with the staff. One thousand eight hundred staff are working there, that's 1,800 families when the chips are down. I retired last February from that, but was asked to work on the World Meeting of Families 2018 for RTÉ.

I was involved in the last Papal visit to Dublin and Galway in 1979. There was huge excitement in the Phoenix Park, you just couldn't describe it adequately. When the Aer Lingus 747 came over the park and dipped its wings and flew around, the cheers and the tears in the crowd, which was about 1.3 million, were incredible.

In Dublin, I was involved in choosing the music that was playing in the Phoenix Park while people were arriving from 5 a.m. There were no CDs at that time, it was all cassettes. There was a lot of music needed!

I also organised the offertory procession, and we told the story of Christianity in Ireland by the places that the participants came from – Tara and Slane, where St Patrick lit the Paschal fire; Glendalough and Clonmacnoise; Kells; and Waterford, where Blessed Edmund Rice funded his first school with a bakery. A child from inner city Dublin, which was a high-crime area, carried up some hosts. Her name was Catherine Traynor, and from the day she was chosen to be involved, there was no crime in that area of the city.

I was also on the committee to organise the Galway Mass. I had the responsibility of making sure the public address system worked in the racecourse, so we had to find a company capable of doing that job for such a large area, as there was no one in Ireland at the time. A man called Harold Smart from Northern England got the job.

My name is Fr Dermod McCarthy, and I was honoured to be one of those commentating for RTÉ at the Papal Mass in the Phoenix Park on Sunday 26 August.

TARA MCGAHAN

When I was planning my summer holidays this year, I had no idea that they would include a unique experience as part of a group of international media who were in Ireland for the visit of Pope Francis for the World Meeting of Families 2018. But, that's exactly what happened on 25 and 26 August when I was invited by the World Meeting of Families 2018 Media and Communications Manager to be part of her team.

Having recently been offered a place on a journalism course in Dublin City University, I grabbed the opportunity with both hands.

There was a total of five media centres in operation for the visit of Pope Francis to Ireland with the main one being in Dublin Castle. I arrived there for 8 a.m. on Saturday 25 August feeling nervous and excited. I had to go through a full security check before I received my official accreditation to be part of the media covering the visit.

I was taken aback by the huge numbers of media in the Dublin Castle media centre (about 1,200 in total from thirty-one countries). There were desks as far as you could see with busy journalists writing and recording. I was taken aback by all the well-known faces who were there from across RTÉ, BBC and UTV. I stood alongside Miriam O'Callaghan, Bryan Dobson and Conor Pope.

I was assigned to the Italian broadcasting company RAI as a runner. The RAI team were accredited as part of a group known as the 'VAMP' – the Vatican Accredited Media Pack. These are a small group of media who travelled to Ireland with Pope Francis on the papal flight and had access to all the venues he was to visit while he was in Ireland. A total of sixty-eight VAMP came to Ireland on the papal flight.

I met up with the RAI TV team in Dublin Castle after their arrival with Pope Francis for his address to authorities, civil society and diplomatic corps. I was straight in at the deep end and was shown how they record and edit TV clips. I helped the cameraman set up for filming and had to ensure that the location we chose was suitable. It

was exciting to watch the crew set up and to see the reporters prepare to go live. It was a unique experience for me to be behind the scenes and I learned so much.

On Saturday evening, I boarded the last media shuttle bus for Croke Park for the Festival of Families event with Pope Francis. We were directed to the level 7 media centre in the Hogan Stand. The place was buzzing with journalists, editors, technicians and more well-known personalities such as Marty Morrissey and Brendan Donohoe. It was incredible to see how much effort goes into everything behind the cameras.

From my position at level 7 in the Hogan Stand, I could see the crowd beginning to build. Broadcasters began going live around the world. As the time approached for Pope Francis to arrive, we were escorted by the media team down to the pitch so as we could access more close up shots of the Pope as he arrived to celebrate with families from across the world.

It was surreal to be standing just a few metres away from Pope Francis as he passed by in a customised golf buggy. He received a wonderful Irish welcome from the crowd of almost eighty-thousand. The Festival of Families event was amazing.

The media and communications team had a debrief afterwards up in level 7 and we received our places and instructions for the Closing Mass the next day. I returned to my accommodation feeling tired but exhilarated, and ready for day two.

I had a really early start again on the Sunday morning. The VAMP were split into two groups – one was bound for Dublin Airport for the flight to Knock and the other, the group I was in, was bound for Phoenix Park. We met at Dublin Castle for a security screen and were given a Garda escort directly to the Phoenix Park where the Mass was to take place.

There was another large media centre in operation for the 1,200 journalists in the Phoenix Park. It was a hive of activity by the time we arrived. The TV crews and photographers were escorted to their positions for the Mass – some were on large media risers (platforms) and others had staged movements accompanied by a press officer and a Garda. I assisted RAI TV with more of their live broadcasts in Italian. Their pictures were colourful and cheerful and showcased a very positive image of Ireland.

The day passed by in a blur of enthusiastic Mass-goers and a busy media centre. The VAMP were moved onto their buses for the airport just before the end of the Mass. They had the return journey home with the Pope. I stayed behind in the Phoenix Park media centre. It was a lot to take in.

There were several media team selfies and pics to record the amazing team I was part of. The entire experience was over in a matter of thirty-six hours, but it was an amazing opportunity. It has really motivated and excited me for my future studies in journalism. Who knows, there may even be a papal visit somewhere in the future where I will be one of the VAMP on the papal flight, sharing the story with the world!

My name is Tara McGahan, and I was a volunteer with the media and communications team for the World Meeting of Families 2018.

I hadn't anticipated the lump in my throat! And yet there it was, unbidden and persistent. As I earnestly attempted to keep my composure, in the background I was aware of the sonorous voice of Patrick Bergin singing out the prophetic words of Leonard Cohen's 'Anthem'. And there, very much in the foreground, was Pope Francis, making his entry through the roaring crowds into the Festival of Families in Croke Park as the whole stadium became electric, amplified by the light of thousands upon thousands of camera flashes. This moment stands still for me in the whole journey to and out of the World Meeting of Families 2018.

My personal journey to the World Meeting of Families 2018 began with an invitation in October 2016 from Bishop Denis Nulty to be the diocesan delegate for Kildare and Leighlin. The next twenty-two months were utterly absorbed by this role. Over those months I got to work with a fantastic group of people from across the diocese on our World Meeting of Families

steering committee, facilitating our own diocesan pathway to August 2018. This pathway was trodden with tremendous generosity and extraordinary levels of commitment and work from parish representatives, secretaries, staff and clergy – all seizing this opportunity in the local Church to deepen our commitment to supporting families and to sharing the gift of the Gospel vision for family life today.

When I think of the World Meeting of Families 2018 and my role in it as both the diocesan delegate and a member of the national liturgy committee for the event, lots of different memories come flooding back. I think of the great teamwork I experienced as part of the organising committee for our picnic day in Punchestown in August 2017 and the incredible energy on the day itself, followed by our Family Fun Day in Carlow College in June 2018. I remember back to the training days for the *Amoris* parish conversations that took place in twenty-eight of our parishes and, again, the time spent

JULIE KAVANAGH

sitting around a table with a group of people preparing those training sessions. It also brings to mind the (personally) slightly daunting task of taking part in two of the actual video recordings!

I think of the many photographs sent to faith development services in the year ahead of the World Meeting of Families 2018 – photos of parish enthronements of the Icon of the Holy Family, of parish blessings of pets and of schoolbags, photos of parish family displays and parish picnics. I can almost physically feel the rain of the day in Knock when we caught a first glimpse of the Icon of the Holy Family and I still feel the deep privilege of accompanying that Icon into the Midlands Prison and the three prayer services shared with the prison community, as well as being with the thousands of primary and secondary school students who prayed before the icon in three churches across the diocese.

The months of preparation for the World Meeting of Families 2018

included monthly trips up and down to Clonliffe where I got to meet with diocesan delegates from across the country. Alongside these meetings were the bi-weekly meetings of the liturgy committee, putting shape on the liturgies for the events. I remember the April training day in Athlone when we got to introduce and pray the Opening Liturgy Evening Prayer to representatives of every diocese on the island and, especially, I remember the wonderful occasion of praying that prayer in a packed Carlow cathedral on 21 August. I often think with gratitude of the tremendous excitement and enthusiasm at the three local rehearsals for over 120 members of the diocesan choir who sang in the RDS and in the Phoenix Park. And of course, I have a stream of wonderful images in my brain from the days in the RDS: meeting so many young families, the oasis of Morning Prayer, the richness of inputs (and the privilege of giving one of them), the energy of the exhibition halls and the communion of this shared space.

But when I think back to that lump in my throat in Croke Park, and explore what that might have been about, I reckon that I was realising that, after all the preparations, I was not only sharing the gift and joy of this moment with eighty thousand other people but, most importantly, I was sharing it with my family. And, as in the Phoenix Park the next day, being with my husband and children, and their aunties, uncles and cousins, ultimately made sense of it all!

My name is Julie Kavanagh, and I was the World Meeting of Families 2018 diocesan delegate for Kildare and Leighlin.

BISHOP DENIS NULTY

We stored our photographs in a green Clarks shoebox in the dining room press. The box was opened when relations called and asked about some lesser known grandaunt or distant cousin. The first photograph taken of me was in Knockerk, probably at the age of three, riding my tricycle. The usual sacramental and graduation moments were also captured on film, but nothing beats that first photograph! In every other one I'm the tall one, standing out in the class group at school or college or at a family gathering.

I'm both the youngest and the tallest! I got my father's genes in height and my mothers in character. I'm the youngest of five, with two brothers, Christy and Leo, and two sisters, Ann and Dolores. My parents are sadly both deceased. Dad died after an illness of about four years in 2006, while Mam slipped away into eternity in 2010. I miss them. Parents are the glue that keeps a family connected with one another. Now we depend on the mobile and in particular WhatsApp. I love my family, each of them means the world to me; but I know that when parents die the family home is simply never going to be the same.

Amoris Laetitia is essentially Pope Francis' love letter to families – all our families, mine and yours. Our World Meeting of Families brought together families from all over the world, from every part of Ireland and many from the family of my own diocese of Kildare and Leighlin. This was the first papal visit I was ever involved with in any intimate way, privileged to serve as a member of the board of the World Meeting of Families. My connection with 1979 was travelling with the local curate, Fr John Brogan, to Ballyrit and singing 'He's Got the Whole World in His Hands'.

As a diocese, we gathered several times in the lead up to the World Meeting of Families. We were the first to venture and share a 'Picnic in Punchestown' at the end of the summer of 2017; later we gathered for a 'Family Fun Day' in the grounds of Carlow College, St Patrick's, at the beginning of the summer of 2018. Many in our diocesan family volunteered, sang in the choir, were present on our KANDLE stand in the RDS, or simply attended the different events in the RDS, the Pro-Cathedral, Croke Park or the Phoenix Park around the World Meeting of Families 2018.

I would love to put as much energy into what we will now get out of the World Meeting as to what we put into it. I think it has put new energy into our conversations at parish level around the family. The parish is, after all, a family of families. I notice a number of our churches in the diocese have erected a family wall with Pope Francis at the centre and family pictures, just like the ones in that old Clarks shoebox at home, covering the family wall. A diocese is a family of parishes, fifty-six in my case - that's fifty-six shoeboxes waiting to be prised open, full of memories of what it means to be family.

Our families are much more like the Simpsons rather than the Waltons. A line that has stayed with me from Pope Francis at the World Meeting of Families 2018 comes from the encounter with young couples, including my nephew and namesake Denis and his fiancée Sinead had with Pope Francis in Dublin's Pro-Cathedral: 'There will be no revolution of love without a revolution of tenderness!'

My name is Bishop Denis Nulty, and I am Bishop of Kildare and Leighlin.

The World Meeting of Families 2018 had been in my diary for a long time before it actually came to happen in Dublin. Once the dates were announced, I had the event on my radar. The week was blocked out in the diary, so I could be present to witness this wonderful experience in our own little country.

Having recently lost both my parents, I was very much aware of the word 'family' at the heart of the title. It made me think more about my family unit. I am the eldest of six, and we had a very strong Catholic upbringing. Faith was very important in our home. The Rosary was recited and Mass was a weekly event and nothing superseded it.

In *Amoris Laetitia*, Pope Francis speaks about the love of a mother and a father: 'Children, once born, begin to receive, along with nourishment and care, the spiritual gift of knowing with certainly that they are loved.' This was certainly true in my family. Both parents encouraged us and guided us in the faith. We had both of them for a long time,

until illness took over and the Lord called them to himself nine months apart, and after fifty-one years of marriage. We also had the privilege of our grandmother living with us. She was also instrumental in our faith journey and encouraged us to use our various gifts for the good of others. Pope Francis, in his address in Croke Park, said, 'Fathers and mothers, grandfathers and grandmothers, children and grandchildren: each and every one of us. All of us are called to find, in our family, our fulfilment in love.' This is what our home was.

We were truly blessed to have had such a wonderful start in life. My faith journey began very early and it has become central to my whole being. At the age of thirteen, I was very much involved in my parish community through music. My faith was very much developed through the wonderful liturgies that were so lucky to have during those early years. My daily work is now faith based and it is from this that I continue to receive true fulfilment and contentment.

The build-up to the World Meeting of Families 2018 involved lots of input from my work life. There were diocesan choir gatherings, a family fun day at Mount Melleray, the Icon of the Holy Family visiting the cathedral in Waterford and many more events as the date grew closer.

My experience at the World Meeting of Families was enriching. The days at the Pastoral Congress in the RDS were full of life – meeting old acquaintances, meeting new people and hearing different speakers on various different topics.

A stand out moment for me was the testimony of Olive Foley as she spoke about losing her beloved husband so suddenly and having to move on through life for her children, cherishing his love in her heart. But it was her strong faith and love of God that was central to the story. Death is something that we all have to face, and Olive's testimony was very enriching from a faith stance.

I became involved in the World Meeting of Families 2018 through my love of sacred music, and participated in the choirs on Friday in the RDS and in the Phoenix Park on the Sunday. Sunday was a special day. I travelled with two of my sisters and we became part of the wider choir that participated on the day. The weeks previous involved lots of rehearsals and meetings so that everything was in order. As I walked along the way to the Phoenix Park I was reminded of the great efforts and sense of endurance that Irish people down through the centuries have shown in the development and practice of the faith. I was conscious of the many 'Mass rocks' in the country when, to keep the faith alive, people travelled great distances under difficult and arduous conditions. I could get the sense of pilgrimage and mission endemic to the Irish psyche. This was a journey of hope, celebration, expectancy, reaching out, mission, commitment and a journey of trust in the future.

As we looked out on the huge crowd that had gathered, we were swept along in wonder and awe as Pope Francis arrived in his Popemobile. My thoughts were varied: 'Will we ever see a pope in Ireland again?'; 'Will the faith in Ireland become stronger as a result of this wonderful week?'; 'How can we bottle the good will of this week and keep it alive as we return to our families, parishes and dioceses?' There was a euphoria around the park that was infectious. People were genuinely happy to participate and profess their faith in a very public way. The wind and the rain did not deter people from being there. Older people walked miles to be there. I had a 3.30 a.m. start so that I wouldn't miss the choir bus! But it didn't matter. This was a lifetime experience and it meant something to me as a Catholic in Ireland today.

Now, as I look back on the gathering, I think about my own siblings and their families. I hope that they will have that enriching gift of faith in their lives that we were blessed to have to carry them through the happy days and the sad days. I hope that they will always have

God at their side just like Olive Foley testified to having.

I hope and pray that the World Meeting of Families 2018 will be the springboard for many of our parishioners and Irish people generally to reignite the smouldering embers of their faith and commitment. Our Church needs strong, committed and involved parishioners to build together a strong unit of faith-practice and from that challenge and commitment our Church will again become a positive beacon for people on their life's journey.

In *Amoris Laetitia*, Pope Francis also says, 'Growing up with brothers and sisters makes for a beautiful experience of caring and helping one another.' This was and still is true for us as a family. We care for one another and look out for one another, even more so now as we thank God every day for our parents and try and live out their legacy. As a family, we were privileged to have the wisdom of our grandmother and the enthusiasm of our parents.

I look back with grace and gratitude for the wonderful faith that was passed onto me from the day I was born. It is a gift that I truly treasure and will continue to treasure. The World Meeting of Families 2018 gave me the joy of acknowledging and thanking God for my family and also the faith family to which I belong.

My name is Mary Dee, and I work for the Diocese of Waterford and Lismore and was involved in many different ways with World Meetings of Families 2018.

SHEENA DARCY

When it was announced that the World Meeting of Families would take place in Ireland in 2018, I was thrilled. Having had many opportunities to attend World Youth Days and two International Eucharistic Congresses over the last eighteen years, I knew the World Meeting of Families would be a grace-filled moment for our Church and our country. Knowing that the Pope usually attend such an event was an extra bonus!

Like most people in Ireland, I was baptised as a baby, made my First Holy Communion aged seven and my Confirmation aged twelve. I grew up always knowing that I was born a week after a very special time in Ireland: the visit of Pope John Paul II in 1979. Weekly Mass and prayer at home were a regular feature for our family and faith wasn't something I ever questioned. However, aged thirteen and in my first year of secondary school, I made a conscious decision to stop attending weekly Mass, though I did go occasionally, to please my mother. I thought, if most of my friends and classmates did not go, why should I? For quite a lot of my late childhood and early teenage years, my mother had been ill and, typically, I placed the blame firmly with God. I had absolutely no concept of him as a loving God. To me, at that time, he was just causing me problems.

At the end of transition year at school in the summer of 1996, a friend invited me to the youth festival in Medjugorje. Much to my parents' surprise, I jumped at the chance to go and it was a pilgrimage that would change my life. There I found a great peace and I began to really know God's love for me. After that experience, I longed to know more about my faith and for several years I was like a sponge soaking up everything I could find out about my faith. It wasn't easy for me to practise my faith as a young person in Dublin, but, being involved with Youth 2000, I soon found myself surrounded by other young people who also practised their Catholic faith with great joy. The faith formation I received and the life-long friendships

I made during my time attending Youth 2000 retreats and prayer groups were some of the greatest blessings in my journey of faith.

God has brought me on an incredible journey over the years and I could fill a book with the adventures!

My name is Sheena Darcy, and since 2014 I have been working as secretary to Bishop Kevin Doran in the Diocese of Elphin. As part of the preparation for the World Meeting of Families 2018, I served as diocesan delegate for the Diocese of Elphin. Meeting regularly with the other delegates and with the incredible World Meeting of Families 2018 team, sharing ideas and passing on information and resources to parishes was a great way of being part of this historic event. I consider it a real privilege to be able to serve God in my daily work but above all I am grateful for the gift of faith he has given me which was nurtured by my parents and reignited through the witness of others.

FATHER ARNOLD ROSNEY

My journey with the World Meeting of Families started in September 2015 while watching the closing Papal Mass from Philadelphia, when, in the presence of the Holy Father, the city of Dublin was chosen as host for the 2018 event. Fast forward to October 2016 and, two weeks following the episcopal ordination of Fintan Monahan as Bishop of Killaloe, I was asked to take on the role as co-ordinator for the preparations for the Diocese of Killaloe. Funnily enough, it was following a parish celebration that I was asked to take on the role, and for me it was entering in some way into the unknown of getting to know the whole diocese and how can we engage families and communities on the road ahead.

If I was to be honest, the event of the World Meeting of Families never jumped out to me like the World Youth Day. At the same time, I saw it as a great opportunity not only to reaffirm our families in faith, but also to encourage parishes in the diocese to build on what is working well and, at the same time, to try new things.

My own family of five sisters and one brother were blessed with wonderful parents who worked hard to give us the tools for right living. With such a large family, at times it wasn't easy, but they worked hard to give us all we needed and at the same time taught us to have a profound respect for ourselves and others. They would remind us to appreciate what we have, and look out for each other.

During our preparations for the World Meeting of Families 2018, my mother, Bridget, died from a stroke, having journeyed with the reality of dialyses for a number of years. She was very kind to so many, not least to us, and it was a somewhat sad coincidence we celebrated her funeral Mass on the feast of St Vincent de Paul (a kind man in his own way). She was very proud of my involvement with the World Meeting of Families 2018 and looked forward to attending in Dublin. But it wasn't to be, sadly.

The preparations for the World Meeting of Families 2018 reconnected me with the simple aspects of family. Family is a blessing, albeit imperfect. It's a place of security and where we reveal who we are. It's a unit unlike no other: it doesn't count the cost, but pulls out all the stops. It brought me back to my younger days when we went out to play; when things were less complicated and life was carefree.

The huge array of pastoral resources was a wonderful way to celebrate family through the eyes of faith, especially at significant family times throughout the year. For me, these resources were, and continue to be, a source of faith connection with the simple yet important aspects of family that in small ways take us from the busyness of life to spending quality time together; for example, sitting together for a meal with gadgets switched off, the importance of remembering and telling the story, and allowing space for God in the home.

Now the World Meeting of Families 2018 has concluded, I see it as just the beginning for faith and family formation, and catechesis in our homes and communities. I believe it's in the small things in life that we connect with the person of Jesus Christ, who asks us to 'put out into the deep' time and time again. When we do cast out those nets and take the risk, extraordinary things unfold.

My name is Fr Arnold Rosney and I am a priest of the Diocese of Killaloe. I was the World Meeting of Families 2018 diocesan delegate for Killaloe.

CARMEL HARRINGTON

I grew up in a Catholic family where faith was part of our everyday lives.

One of my earliest childhood memories is my mother whispering the child's prayer to my siblings and I as she tucked us into bed each night:

There are four corners on my bed,
There are four angels overhead,
Matthew, Mark, Luke and John,
God bless this bed that I lay on.

As there were four of us – Fiona, John, Michelle and me – and we believed that we had one angel each to protect us. You know, if I hear those words now, I can feel the blanket of love from my mother.

My parents, Mike and Tina, were both hard workers. Our home was a busy one with all of us constantly on the go. But Sundays were a day of rest. A cooked breakfast, followed by Mass, then home for a roast with all the trimmings were pretty much written in stone. Then we'd watch whatever Sunday matinee was on, which seemed to feature John Wayne a lot back then!

It sounds idyllic and you know what? I think it was.

We went to a Catholic national school where the Angelus was said at 12 p.m. every day. If I hear the scrape of a chair as it's pulled back on a tiled floor now, it brings me back to that time. First Confession, Communion and Confirmation were rites of passage for each of us too, treated with respect and awe, with a good dash of excitement thrown in. Because, of course, all rites of passages came with parties in our family. I went to school at the Loreto convent in Wexford at a time when nuns were all still in residence. They wore the habit and taught classes.

We gave up sweets for Lent every year, believed in the magical powers of a lit candle, prayed to St Anthony when we lost anything and never ate meat on a Friday. My mother is a firm believer in the power of holy water and whenever one of us kids gets a new car or moves into a new house we know that the first gift we'll receive from her is a bottle of Knock's finest.

So many of my childhood and family memories are linked to our faith and the rituals that formed part of that.

I became a lapsed Catholic in my twenties when I left home and started a new chapter in my life in Dublin. My Mass attendance was hit or miss. My parents weren't happy about this, but they never put pressure on me to go back and I respect that. Because, with time, as I got older, I found myself drawn to the Church once more. My husband, Roger, and I, with our two children, Amelia (8) and Nate (7), go to Mass in Screen village as often as we can. We are a small community, where pretty much every one knows each other. And that community, that kinship in Screen, is linked to our faith too. We're lucky, because our parish priest, Fr Denis Kelly, is not only a good man and a friend, he gives good sermons too! Always entertaining, but with a salient, wise centre to each story.

I try to live my life with kindness and, for me, family is everything. So when we heard about the World Meeting of Families 2018 from Fr Denis, it seemed like the perfect event for us to attend. To our delight, we managed to get Festival of Families tickets not just for ourselves, but for my parents too. We decided to leave early, park up and have lunch together before we made our way to Croke Park.

There was great excitement as we made our way onto the pitch and whoops from all when we realised we had 'the good seats'! Mum, Amelia and I saved a nun who had managed to lock herself into one of the portaloos, which we still giggle about now. The concert was wonderful with a mix of community choirs and celebrity performances. When Pope Francis made his way into the stadium on his mini Popemobile, he was about ten feet from us. We could almost touch him. And sharing that moment, watching how happy that made my parents in particular, will never leave me. A personal highlight of the night was Andrea Bocelli singing Ave Maria. Nate had fallen asleep in my arms at this stage, as it was late in the evening and dark. Along with thousands of others, Amelia waved a light from my mobile phone in time to Andrea's beautiful song. It was joyful, emotional and unforgettable. I was filled with love for my family, those beside me in the stadium and those at home too.

My name is Carmel Harrington. I live in Sreen, Co. Wexford with my family. I'm an author, wife, mother, daughter, sister and friend, and my family was one of the many families who took great joy in being part of the World Meeting of Families 2018 in Dublin!